PSYCHE

VICTOR CHATTERJEE

BlueRoseONE.com
Stories Matter
NewDelhi • London

BLUEROSE PUBLISHERS
India | U.K.

BlueRose ONE
Stories Matter
NewDelhi • London

For permissions requests or inquiries regarding this publication, please contact:

BLUEROSE PUBLISHERS
www.BlueRoseONE.com
info@bluerosepublishers.com
+91 8882 898 898
+4407342408967

ISBN: 978-93-7018-854-9

Cover Design: Aman Sharma
Typesetting: Pooja Sharma

First Edition: May 2025

Dedication

To the ones who gave me life –

My Parents – who laid the foundation of every dream, every struggle, every rise.

Your sacrifices are the unseen roots of every chapter written here.

This journey is your legacy, too.

To the ones who gave me my *superpower* –

My Wife, Jayeeta Chatterjee,

My Daughter, Vedanshi, and

My Son, Trivid –

You are not just my family.

You are my fuel, my faith, my fiercest why.

Every word I bled into these pages carries a piece of your light.

To the warriors holding this book in their hands –

Students dreaming beyond grades.

Teachers shaping minds beyond textbooks.

Parents daring to love without conditions.

Billionaires seeking meaning beyond wealth.

And every human in every corner of the world who still believes that healing is not weakness – it's **warrior work**.

This book is for you.

A reminder that **your story is not finished**.

A mirror that says:

"You were always enough. You were always powerful. You were always meant to be unstoppable."

Thank you for daring to walk this path.

The world doesn't need more noise.

It needs your **truth** – spoken out loud, lived out loud.

And if you ever forget,

turn back to these pages –

and remember what it feels like to be **home inside yourself.**

With all my fire, all my flaws, and all my faith,

Victor Chatterjee

Acknowledgements

First and foremost, I am deeply grateful to my parents and my superpowers, my wife, daughter, and son, whose unwavering love, sacrifices, and belief in me have been the silent strength behind every word in this book. You've not only nurtured my mind but protected my soul through every storm. You are my first teachers, my first believers, and forever my home.

I also wish to thank the incredible **Dr.** Carol S. Dweck, whose groundbreaking work on mindsets reshaped the trajectory of my thinking – and my life. Your words planted the seeds of growth in moments when all I saw was rock bottom. You reminded me that the mind isn't fixed – it's a force, and it can evolve.

To those who inspired me with compassion, challenged me with intellect, and uplifted me through encouragement – your energy lives in every chapter of this book.

And now... to **you** – yes, the ones who belittled, mocked, dismissed, and ridiculed me.

You – with your polished cruelty, passive-aggressive smirks, and carefully curated doubt – thought you were writing the final chapter of my confidence.

You almost did.

But instead, you gave me something far more potent than approval: **resilience**.

Thank you for the public humiliation, the whispered sabotage, the deliberate exclusions, and the way you weaponised words as if they were in your native tongue.

You lit a fire in me that your dialect of negativity could never douse.

You tried to bury me – but forgot I was a seed.

So, to all of you who thought your toxicity would break me: *you're in this book too.*

But not in the way you hoped.

You're the villains of the origin story that gave rise to a voice louder than your silence, stronger than your ridicule, and wiser than your ignorance.

And finally, to every reader who has ever been made to feel "less than" – this book is for you.

Let them doubt you. Then let them watch.

Preface

To those who feel deeply, think restlessly, and rise relentlessly.

There was a time in my life – not long ago – when I questioned everything.

Not just the path I had taken or the goals I was chasing but even my own **worth, identity, and capacity to feel whole.** I had checked every societal box – education, career, family, reputation. And yet, I felt incomplete. Not because I lacked, but because something in me was unheard, unexplored, and unhealed.

That something is what this book is about.

PSYCHE was born not out of convenience or ambition but out of necessity – a deep, unrelenting need to understand why we feel what we feel and do what we do and how we can finally **reclaim agency over our minds and emotions.** This book is as much a product of my academic pursuit as it is of my lived experiences: my wins, my traumas, my silent battles, and my breakthroughs.

At the age of 38, with over **14 years in the tech and consulting world**, working inside the complex systems of multinational software enterprises, I began noticing a different kind of system failure – not in code, but in people. **Brilliant minds collapsing under emotional weight. Talented individuals doubting themselves into silence. Leaders crumbling behind closed doors.** And in the mirror – someone who, despite every "success", felt like an imposter in his own narrative.

That's when I dived headfirst into psychology. Not as a casual reader. As a desperate explorer.

Books led to therapy. Therapy led to journaling. Journaling led to research. Research led to writing. Writing became this book.

What You'll Discover Inside

PSYCHE is a journey – not a lecture. It's written not to impress, but to **connect**. Each chapter is crafted with the goal of guiding you through **the architecture of human behaviour**, emotional intelligence, mindset transformation, and the subtle forces that shape our lives.

This book is for you if:

- You've ever **felt emotions you couldn't name.**
- You've **doubted your worth**, despite external validation.
- You've tried to grow but feel stuck in **behavioural loops.**
- You want to understand yourself **and others more deeply.**
- You believe in the power of **personal evolution.**

The chapters are structured with a mix of **psychological theory, real-life anecdotes, case studies, diagrams**, and **reflections**. You'll meet not just the concepts, but the *characters* who bring them to life – including learnings from my own story.

Why This Book Matters Now

We live in a time of **emotional overload and cognitive burnout**. Teenagers are battling identity crises. Parents are parenting from pain. Teachers are teaching without being taught how to regulate their own stress. Millionaires are feeling empty. Billionaires are asking therapists what joy feels like. Algorithms know us better than we know ourselves – and yet, we are still **mysteries to our own minds**.

This book is my response to that crisis.

We need more than motivation. We need **insight**.

We need more than hacks. We need **healing**.

We need more than theory. We need **tools**.

That's what *PSYCHE* offers.

● Who This Book Is For

It's for:

- The **B-school student** trying to find confidence in boardrooms.
- The **teacher** losing sleep over a child they can't reach.
- The **teenager** who doesn't know who they are yet.
- The **parent** repeating cycles they swore they'd end.
- The **billionaire** feeling disconnected from meaning.
- The **ordinary person** with extraordinary potential

No matter where you are in life, this book will speak to your mind – and whisper to your heart.

❖ One Last Thought Before You Begin

You may come to this book looking for knowledge.

But I hope you leave with something far greater – **understanding.**

Because once you understand yourself, no one can define you again.

Once you understand your mind, you stop being a prisoner of it.

And once you understand your psyche, you begin to master your life.

So, open this book not just with your eyes – open it with your curiosity. Your courage. Your chaos.

Let's begin.

~ Victor Chatterjee

Kolkata, India

Year 2025

Introduction

"To explore the human psyche is not to decode a machine — it is to enter a universe."

There's a storm happening within you right now.

Maybe it's quiet. Maybe it's thunderous. But it's there — swirling behind your eyes, pulsing behind your actions, whispering behind your decisions. It's the storm of your **emotions**, your **thoughts**, your **memories**, your **doubts**, your **beliefs**, and your **fears** — all dancing together to form the mystery that is *you*.

We wake up every day and step into the world assuming we know who we are. We put on clothes, wear our names, scroll through our lives, and play our roles — but how many of us truly understand the **architecture of our inner world**?

We know how to charge a phone. We know how to drive a car.

But how many of us know how to **regulate our mind**?

How many of us know why we snap at the ones we love, freeze in moments that matter, or feel empty after chasing everything we were told would fulfil us?

This book was written because I didn't have those answers either.

- **This is Not a Psychology Textbook**

Let's get that straight. You're not holding a dusty academic journal. This isn't a collection of dry definitions and complex jargon meant to be quoted in exams and forgotten in life.

This book is alive. It breathes. It bleeds.

It's built for **real people with real struggles** — who feel lost in their thoughts, overwhelmed by their emotions, and unsure if they're broken... or just human.

Every chapter in *PSYCHE* is a doorway into a **dimension of yourself.** And every insight is meant to take you deeper – not just into knowledge, but into **awareness**. You'll read things here that will make you pause mid-sentence and whisper to yourself, *"Wait... that's me."*

You'll see your childhood reflected. Your relationships exposed. Your beliefs challenged. And your potential awakened.

❖ **The Human Mind Is Not a System. It's a story.**

Every behaviour you exhibit has a root. Every emotion you feel has a map.

What you fear, what you avoid, what you chase – it all comes from somewhere. And until you explore it, **you'll keep living the same loops, calling it fate.**

Have you ever asked yourself:

- Why do I react the way I do when I feel disrespected?
- Why do certain memories haunt me even after years?
- Why do I self-sabotage right before things get good?
- Why do I find it hard to trust, to let go, to forgive, or to feel enough?

The answers aren't random. They're coded into your psyche – and in this book, we're decoding that **not with judgement, but with compassion.**

❖ **Tools, Not Just Thoughts**

You'll find powerful tools throughout this book:

- Frameworks that explain behaviour with **clarity**
- Real-life case studies that make abstract ideas **relatable**
- Reflection prompts that force you to **pause and go inward.**
- Diagrams that simplify the most complex emotional patterns

But most importantly, you'll find a **voice** – mine – that speaks not from a pedestal but from beside you.

Because I'm not a guru. I'm not here to impress you.

I'm here to walk with you – through the darkness and into clarity.

❖ From Boardrooms to Bedrooms – This Book Speaks to All

You might be a student trying to find confidence.

A parent wondering how to stop repeating the trauma you swore you wouldn't pass on.

A teacher exhausted by systems that crush creativity.

A leader who feels powerful on the outside but empty within.

A teenager lost in a world of filters and false identities.

Or someone who looks like they "have it all" but feels like something's missing.

This book is for you.

It's not about fixing you – because you are **not broken**.

It's about helping you understand the systems, stories, and scars that shaped you – so you can reclaim your power.

❖ A Brutal Truth

Let me offer a truth most books won't say:

You can't grow until you stop lying to yourself.

And most of us have been lying for years. About our happiness. Our control. Our relationships. Our past. Our worth. We wear masks so long, we forget who we were before we needed them.

This book doesn't ask you to pretend. It invites you to **strip down the emotional armour** and look at yourself in the raw. That's where the transformation begins.

❖ Written from Fire, Not Theory

I didn't write this because I'm perfect. I wrote this because I was broke.

I've faced toxic environments, seen confidence eroded by people's words, been humiliated, dismissed, and underestimated – and at times, emotionally destroyed.

But from those ashes, I studied. I read. I healed. I grew.

I turned wounds into wisdom. Pain into pages. And now, you're holding the result.

You'll feel it in the chapters – the rage, the reflection, the redemption.

You'll know this book was not manufactured. It was **lived.**

❖ What Comes Next

Here's how we'll walk this journey together:

1. You'll learn the **science** of human behaviour.
2. You'll reflect on your **own story.**
3. You'll challenge your **mental patterns.**
4. You'll learn to regulate your **emotions.**
5. You'll master your **mindset and responses.**
6. You'll be empowered to **rewrite your narrative.**
7. You'll begin to **influence your world** – not just react to it.

By the end, you won't just understand the human psyche.

You'll understand **your own** – in a way you never have before.

❖ One Last Thing Before We Dive In

If at any point during this book you feel exposed, emotional, or even uncomfortable – *good*. That means it's working.

Because the greatest breakthroughs don't come from comfort.

They come when we finally look at ourselves without flinching.

So, take a deep breath. Open your heart. Quiet the noise.

And let's step into the deepest story ever written: **your own mind.**

Welcome to PSYCHE.

Let's begin.

~ Victor Chatterjee

Kolkata, India

Year 2025

Contents

Chapter 1: Foundations of Human Behaviour

"Human behaviour flows from three main sources: desire, emotion, and knowledge." – Plato

❖ *Welcome to the Interior World*

You are not just a name. Not just a face. Not just a LinkedIn title, a job role, or a family label.

You are a constellation of memories.

A symphony of chemicals.

A sculpture shaped by experience.

A battlefield of thought vs. emotion.

A living narrative – constantly rewritten, often without your awareness.

So, here's the first truth this book wants to shatter wide open:

Human behaviour is not random. It's not irrational. It's not mysterious.

It is **rooted, patterned, logical**, and **predictable** – *if* you know where to look.

❖ The Biological Blueprint: You Were Wired Before You Were Woken

Before you ever spoke a word...

Before you made your first decision...

Before you even formed a memory...

Your brain had already begun building your behavioural future.

Inside the womb, your neural circuits were forming. Your genes were whispering their coded instructions. Your **temperament** – your natural baseline of emotional reactivity – was already taking shape.

❖ **Think about this:**

Why are some babies calm, while others scream at the flicker of light?

Why do some children show courage and others panic at the sound of a stranger's voice?

Because biology isn't optional. It's foundational.

Our **genetic makeup** determines much of our behaviour – not in absolutes, but in tendencies. It decides:

- How easily we get emotionally activated.
- How fast we recover from stress.
- Whether we are novelty seekers or safety cravers
- Our natural threshold for pleasure, anxiety, attention, and even empathy

❖ **Scientific Note:** The limbic system – particularly the **amygdala** – is already functioning by the time you're a newborn. It begins determining what you perceive as "threat" vs "safe" *before* you can rationally process the world.

But here's where it gets fascinating...

❖ 1.2 Environment: The Sculptor of Potential

If biology gives us the **clay**, the environment becomes the **sculptor**.

Imagine two identical seeds. One is planted in fertile soil with sunlight and clean water. The other is buried under concrete. Would we ever blame the second seed for not blooming?

We are all born with potential – but our **upbringing, relationships, and early environments** decide what parts of us flourish... and what parts wither.

❖ **The Power of Parenting:**

- Parents who validate emotions raise children who regulate emotions.
- Parents who criticise constantly raise children who self-criticise endlessly.
- Neglect breeds emotional starvation. Presence breeds emotional resilience.

📺 **The Impact of Observation:**

Children are the most advanced **behavioural mimicry machines** on the planet. They absorb **tone, expression, conflict style**, and even **emotional vocabulary** from their surroundings.

They don't learn by being told. They learn by watching you.

❖ 1.3 The Mirror Neurone Revolution: We Feel What We See

"We are wired to connect." – Dr Dan Siegel

Your brain contains **mirror neurones** – a system that allows you to *feel* what others feel, *imitate* what others do, and **absorb emotional patterns** even without words.

That's why:

- A baby cries when another baby cries.
- You wince when you see someone get hurt.
- You start talking like your coworkers after a few months on the job.

This is also why **toxic environments are dangerous**: not just to your body, but to your brain. You don't just survive them. **You become them.**

Jaw-Dropper Insight: Most people's self-talk is the voice of someone who once hurt them. That voice became the internal narrator – because that's what mirror neurones do.

1.4 Cognition: Thoughts Aren't Facts – But We Believe Them Anyway

Now let's go deeper.

Imagine two people are ignored in a meeting.

One thinks, "*They must be busy.*"

The other thinks, "*I'm invisible. I don't matter.*"

Same moment. Different meaning. Different **emotional consequence.**

Why? Because of **cognitive filters.**

These are the **belief systems** – formed from past experiences – that determine how you interpret the world.

For example:

- Someone who was emotionally neglected may see distance as *rejection.*
- Someone who was abused may see intensity as *normal.*
- Someone who was bullied may interpret silence as *disapproval.*

And unless we challenge these filters, we start calling them "truth".

Behavioural Law: Your interpretation of reality shapes your emotional reaction to it – far more than the actual event.

1.5 Culture & Social Programming: The Unseen Puppet Master

Culture is invisible – until you try to step outside it.

What we call "normal behaviour" is often just **a script written by our society**. Culture tells us:

- When to speak
- How to love
- What does success look like?
- Who we are allowed to be.

It decides which emotions are "acceptable" and which are "taboo".

Some cultures reward stoicism. Others honour emotional expression. Some suppress grief. Others celebrate it.

And without realising it, we internalise these codes so deeply that we think they're our own thoughts.

🔍 **Ask Yourself**: Do I believe this... or was I *taught* to believe this?

⚔ 1.6 Nature vs Nurture: A Dialogue, Not a Debate

Here's what most people get wrong:

It's not *nature vs. nurture.*

It's **Nature in conversation with Nurture.** Constantly. Continuously. Intimately.

Example:

- A child born with a high sensitivity gene may become anxious in a chaotic home – or artistic in a nurturing one.
- A naturally impulsive child may thrive under structured guidance – or spiral in an unpredictable environment.

Your biology **sets the stage**, but your environment **writes the script** – unless you become the author yourself.

👬 1.7 Case Study: Rahul & Aryan – Same House, Different Hearts

Meet **Rahul** and **Aryan.** Twin brothers. Same house. Same parents.

But by age 18, their personalities couldn't be more different.

Rahul was introspective, calm, and high-achieving.

Aryan was defiant, explosive, and constantly seeking validation.

Why?

Because **Rahul interpreted emotional distance as freedom** – while **Aryan saw it as abandonment.**

The difference wasn't the environment. It was the **internal narrative** each child constructed. The filters. The thoughts. The expectations. The coping.

💡 Lesson: Two people can go through the same experience – and walk away with two completely different emotional realities.

🧘 1.8 Pause & Reflect:

- What behaviours do I exhibit repeatedly – and where did they come from?
- Am I reacting to my present – or reenacting my past?
- Who are the voices in my head when I'm under stress? Are they mine?

📌 Chapter Summary:

Human behaviour is a tapestry of biology, emotion, experience, and belief.

You weren't born broken – you were built in layers. And you can rebuild, piece by piece.

Chapter 2: Cognition and Emotion — An Intertwined Journey

"Your emotions are the slaves to your thoughts, and you are the slave to your emotions." – *Elizabeth Gilbert*

A Battle You Fight Every Day — Without Realising It

Have you ever sat in silence after a text that never came, convincing yourself someone doesn't care?

Or stood in front of a crowd, heart racing, wondering, *why do I suddenly feel like I'm not enough?*

Or lay awake at 3 a.m., replaying every word from a meeting that happened 6 days ago?

That, right there, is the war between your **thoughts** and your **emotions.**

Cognition is how you process the world.

Emotion is how you *feel* the world.

And here's the revelation:

They're not enemies. They're **dance partners** – constantly moving together, misstepping, improvising, leading, and reacting. When they synchronise, you thrive. When they clash, you spiral. resonance.

2.1 The Myth of Rationality — You Are Not a Logic Machine

"Man is not a rational animal; he is a rationalising one." – *Robert Heinlein*

We love to believe we are rational creatures, guided by logic, facts, and data.

We imagine ourselves as thinkers who feel – when in truth, we are **feelers who think.**

From the moment we wake up, our brains are flooded with **sensory inputs, emotional impressions**, and **unconscious associations** long before our rational mind kicks in.

When you choose a shirt in the morning, you may think it's about colour or professionalism – but it's often about **how you want to feel**. Confident. Safe. Sharp. Validated.

You think you made a **choice.**

But often, you had a **feeling** and then built a logical story around it.

🎯 **The truth?** Your emotions are the architects of your decisions. Your logic just decorates the walls.

🔬 **What the Brain Says:**

Neurologist **António Damásio** discovered something astounding:

People who suffered damage to the parts of the brain responsible for emotion **could not make even the simplest decisions** – like what to eat.

Without emotion, there was **no preference, no urgency, and no desire.**

They were stuck in infinite logic loops – because **emotion gives logic its direction.**

So, when someone says, *"Don't be emotional – be logical,"*

They're ignoring the fact that **emotion is the engine.** Logic is just the GPS.

🔁 2.2 The Thought-Emotion Loop – How One Triggers the Other

"You don't feel the way you feel because of what happened. You feel the way you feel because of what you told yourself about what happened."

Let's break down the **most important emotional cycle** most people don't know they live in:

🔄 **The Loop:**

1. **A Thought Appears:**
2. *"I'm not doing enough."*
3. **The Body Responds:**
4. You feel tightness in your chest. A rush of anxiety. Your stomach churns.
5. **That Feeling Triggers More Thoughts:**
6. *"I'm falling behind. Everyone else has it together."*
7. **Which Deepens the Emotion:**
8. Now it's not just anxiety. It's panic. Shame. Defeat.
9. **And Then You Act:**
10. You procrastinate. Or overwork. Or shut down. Or scroll Instagram numbly.

This is the **thought-emotion loop.**

It **feeds itself** unless interrupted with awareness and conscious reframing.

🧠 And the kicker? This entire loop can happen in less than **three seconds.**

The most dangerous part is – we think this loop is truth.

But it's not. It's a habit. Mental muscle memory. Neuro-emotional scripting.

Once you **see it**, you can **step outside it**. That's where freedom begins.

2.3 Emotions Are Data — Not Directives

Your emotions are **not flaws** in your system. They are **signals** — your internal GPS trying to communicate something important.

Yet, we've been conditioned to:

- **Deny** them: "I shouldn't feel this way."
- **Shame** them: "I'm too sensitive."
- **Worship** them: "If I feel it, it must be true."

But there's a wiser path: **listen to them without obeying them.**

Think of emotions like dashboard warning lights:

- **Anger** = "Something feels unfair."
- **Anxiety** = "There's uncertainty or perceived danger."
- **Sadness** = "You've lost something meaningful."
- **Joy** = "Your needs are being met."

Each emotion is a **call to investigate.** Not to suppress. Not to explode.

Just to understand.

"Feelings are visitors. Let them come and go, but don't hand them the keys to your house."

2.4 The Hidden Architect — Core Beliefs

Imagine your mind like a skyscraper.

- The **top floors** are your everyday thoughts.
- The **lobby** is your current mood.
- But deep in the **foundation**, buried beneath memory and identity, are your **core beliefs.**

These are **not thoughts you choose.** They're conclusions you *absorbed* long ago — from experiences, carers, culture, or trauma.

Common Core Beliefs:

- "I am not enough."
- "I must be perfect to be loved."
- "People always leave."
- "If I show weakness, I will be hurt."
- "I don't deserve good things."

Once these beliefs are installed, your mind starts interpreting the world to **prove them right**.

This is called **confirmation bias** – your psyche searches for evidence to support its deepest belief. Even if that belief is harming you.

🔍 **Example:**

Your boss forgets to respond to your email.

- If your core belief is *"I'm invisible"*,
- → You feel rejected, insignificant.
- If your belief is *"People are busy – it's not personal"*,
- → You feel understanding and neutral.

Two people. Same event. Two emotional realities.

The difference? **Belief.**

And until you uncover, examine, and update these beliefs, your life becomes a loop of emotional déjà vu.

🌀 2.5 Case Study: Nisha's Spiral – When the Past Shapes the Present

Nisha was a top performer in her company.

Brilliant. Disciplined. But one minor correction from her manager would send her into **emotional chaos**.

She'd replay the comment for days. Lose sleep. Question her competence.

In therapy, she traced the emotion back to childhood. Her father only acknowledged her **when she excelled**. Love was tied to achievement. Criticism was rejection.

So even now, as a 34-year-old professional, Nisha was **not responding to her boss**.

She was responding to her father – **through the lens of her 7-year-old self.**

🔦 Emotional triggers are time machines. They transport you back to the moment the wound was made.

But once she **realised the loop**, she began to pause. Challenge the story. Reframe.

That is healing.

🔍 2.6 Emotional Reasoning – The Lie That Feels True

"If I feel it, it must be true." ← This is the most dangerous logic in emotional life.

Let's break this down.

When you feel shame, you assume you must be **bad.**

When you feel fear, you assume there must be **danger**.

When you feel anger, you assume someone is **guilty**.

But emotions are **not facts**.

They are **data** – influenced by:

- Past trauma
- Sleep quality
- Hunger
- Hormonal fluctuations

- Unspoken fears
- Cognitive distortions

The mistake is not feeling.

The mistake is **letting the feeling dictate the truth** without investigation.

Emotion: "I feel like I'm failing."

Awareness: "Let me ask – is that a fact, or is that fear speaking?"

2.7 Emotional Granularity – Vocabulary for the Soul

There's a big difference between saying:

- "I feel bad."
- and
- "I feel rejected, overlooked, ashamed, and tense."

This is **emotional granularity** – the ability to identify and articulate emotions with **precision**.

Why It Matters:

- Granularity helps regulate emotion.
- It builds empathy and communication.
- It helps **prevent emotional explosions** caused by unidentified overwhelm.

Children taught to name emotions grow up with better:

- Conflict resolution
- Self-esteem
- Resilience
- Social intelligence

As adults, most of us still walk around saying, *"I'm fine,"* when we're fractured.

✍ Try this:

When you feel "bad" – stop. Ask yourself:

- Is this disappointment?
- Is this sadness?
- Is this regret?
- Is this exhaustion?
- Is this grief?

Each answer leads to a different kind of self-care.

2.8 The Cycle of Cognitive Healing

"You do not become free by fighting the darkness. You become free by turning on the light."

Let's get something straight before we begin:

You are not broken.

You are layered.

And healing is not about becoming someone new – it's about remembering who you were before the world taught you to doubt yourself.

Every thought you've repeated for years...

Every emotion you feel reflexively...

Every story your mind plays on loop like background music in your daily life...

All of it can be rewired – *but only if you're brave enough to step into awareness.*

This is not self-help fluff.

This is **neuroplasticity** in action.

This is **inner rewiring** at a cognitive, emotional, and narrative level.

Let's walk through the five stages of the healing cycle that reshapes your psyche – not just temporarily, but fundamentally.

Step 1: Awareness – Shine a Light on the Pattern

You cannot change what you cannot see.

Healing begins with becoming aware of the loops you're stuck in. The behaviours you justify. The emotions you suppress. The thoughts you mistake for truth.

Ask yourself:

- What do I keep doing... that keeps hurting me?
- What situations do I keep attracting... or avoiding?
- What emotional responses feel automatic and overwhelming?

"Awareness is the first act of power. It does not change you – but it gives you the keys to the cage."

This step isn't about fixing anything yet. It's just about **noticing**. Watching your inner world like a scientist. Curious. Compassionate. Conscious.

Step 2: Acceptance – Don't Fight the Feeling. Feel It Fully.

Most of us resist what we're ashamed of.

But here's the paradox of emotional healing:

What you **resist** persists.

What you **accept** transforms.

Acceptance doesn't mean you approve of the pain.

It means you stop running from it long enough to understand it.

Instead of saying:

- "I shouldn't feel this way."
- "Why am I still like this?"

- "I thought I was over this..."

Say this:

- "This emotion has a reason for being here."
- "I am allowed to feel this. It doesn't define me."
- "This pain is a messenger, not a monster."

Let the emotion in. Let it speak. Then let it go.

Step 3: Inquiry – Find the Root of the Thought

Once you've observed the pattern and sat with the emotion, it's time to **interrogate the thought behind it.**

This is where the real magic begins. You start becoming a detective of your own mind.

Let's say the thought is:

"I'm always going to be alone."

Ask:

- "Where did I first hear this?"
- "When did I start believing this?"
- "Is this thought coming from a recent experience – or an old wound?"
- "Is this my voice – or someone else's I internalised?"

Often, you'll trace it back to:

- A parent's criticism
- A childhood memory of rejection
- A traumatic moment you never processed.

You are not your thoughts.

You are the thinker of your thoughts – and that means you have the power to **question, unlearn, and rewrite** them.

Step 4: Reframing – Choose a New Truth

Here's where the shift happens.

Once you've exposed the lie or distortion in the old thought, it's time to replace it with something **truer**, **healthier**, and **empowering** – something you can build your future on.

This is called **cognitive reframing.**

Old Thought:

"I'm not enough. No one really cares."

New Reframe:

"I may not feel enough right now – but I am learning, healing, and growing. My worth is not defined by others' validation."

Old Thought:

"If I make a mistake, I'll be judged and rejected."

New Reframe:

"Mistakes are how I learn. My value is not tied to perfection."

Reframing is not about **lying to yourself.**

It's about **choosing thoughts that align with your future, not your fear.**

Bonus Reframing Tool: "What else could be true?"

Whenever you feel stuck in a painful narrative, pause and ask:

"What else could be true here?"

It opens the door to possibility.

- Maybe they didn't ignore you – maybe they were overwhelmed.
- Maybe you weren't abandoned – maybe someone else didn't know how to love.
- Maybe your fear is real – but so is your strength.

This simple question creates **cognitive spaciousness** – and from that space, healing begins.

💪 Step 5: Practice – Healing Happens in Repetition

Let's be real: **one insight doesn't change a life.**

Transformation happens in **micro-decisions** repeated over time.

Every time you catch a negative thought and pause...

Every time you sit with an emotion instead of numbing it...

Every time you rewrite the old story in real time...

You are laying down new neural pathways.

That's not a metaphor. That's **neuroscience.**

🧠 Your brain rewires based on **what you repeat.**

So, create rituals. Set reminders. Write your new truths on sticky notes. Surround yourself with people who reinforce your healing – not your history.

Healing isn't a straight line. It's a spiral.

You'll revisit old wounds. But each time, with more strength, clarity, and grace.

The Cycle of Healing in One Sentence:

Awareness invites clarity. Acceptance makes space. Inquiry reveals the lie. Reframing speaks the truth. And practice rewrites the story.

You are not here to be fixed.

You are here to become **fully, fiercely, and freely yourself** – with a mind that serves you, not sabotages you.

🧘 2.9 Pause & Reflect.

"The moment you stop running from yourself is the moment you begin coming home."

This section isn't just a list of questions. It's a **mirror.**

You don't need to rush. In fact, if you feel an urge to skip this part – *pause longer.* That's your psyche resisting what might be the most important truths you haven't said aloud yet.

These questions aren't here to fix you.

They're here to **invite you back into yourself.**

So, take a breath.

Put your phone on silent.

Sit up. Close your eyes for a moment. Then read on.

1. What emotions visit me the most? And how do they show up in my body?

Is it anxiety? Does it crawl up your chest like a rising tide before a storm?

Is it anger? Does it burn in your jaw, your fists, your voice?

Is it sadness? Does it settle like a quiet fog behind your eyes?

Our emotions are not floating concepts – they **live in the body.**

They are the language of your nervous system. Learn to feel their footsteps.

Reflect:

- When do these emotions most often appear?
- Who or what seems to activate them?
- What am I usually thinking when this emotion arises?

2. What thoughts am I mistaking for truth?

Remember: a thought is just that – a **thought.**

Not a prophecy. Not a fact. Not a reflection of your worth.

Yet most of us accept certain thoughts as absolute:

- "I'll never be good enough."

- “Everyone eventually leaves.”
- “I always mess up when it matters.”
- “No one truly sees me.”

Where did these begin?

Can you trace them back to a person, a moment, a voice from your past?

Challenge: Write down your top 3 recurring negative thoughts – and ask:

Whose voice is this? Is it mine... or someone else’s I’ve internalised?

💔 3. What belief about myself am I unknowingly carrying into every interaction?

This is the core. The operating system.

Are you carrying the belief that:

- You’re unworthy of love?
- You’re only valued for what you produce?
- You are not allowed to fail?
- You must be strong at all costs?

These beliefs sit silently behind your decisions, your defences, and your doubts.

They become the **lens** through which you see the world – and they often distort reality.

“You don’t see things as they are. You see them as *you* are.”

Ask yourself:

- What belief is at the root of my emotional pain?
- What belief is driving my perfectionism, my silence, my anger, or my withdrawal?

🧨 4. When I feel triggered, what is the real story I'm telling myself?

A trigger is not about what happened – it's about **what it meant to you.**

Let's say someone ignores your message.

The trigger isn't the silence. It's the *interpretation*:

"They're abandoning me. I'm not important. I'm being erased."

That's not about them. That's about your internal story.

Break it down:

- What happened?
- What did I feel?
- What story did I instantly attach to that feeling?
- Is that story *always* true?

Rewrite the story:

"Maybe they were busy. Maybe this has nothing to do with my worth. I can choose a different meaning."

✨ 5. If I treated my emotions like a child, what would I say to them right now?

This is one of the most healing questions you'll ever ask.

Your anger? It's a child trying to be heard.

Your fear? A child looking for safety.

Your shame? A child hiding from rejection.

Your job? A child bursting to be let out again.

Visualise this:

Imagine your emotion sitting beside you, in the form of your younger self – 6 or 7 years old.

What would you say to them?

Would you scold them? Or would you hold them?

Speak to your emotions like someone you love — not someone you're trying to silence.

6. What if the version of me I'm trying to hide... is the key to my healing?

We all have a shadow — the part of ourselves we disown.

- The part that's "too sensitive".
- "Too loud"
- "Too needy"
- "Too angry"
- "Too soft"
- "Too weird"

We buried those parts to fit in. To survive. To be loved.

But often, **those exact traits** are the most beautiful, necessary, and powerful parts of who we are.

Dare to ask:

What part of me have I hidden to be accepted... and what has that cost me?

Final Reflection:

Now take a moment to breathe. Place your hand on your chest.

Feel your heartbeat — that steady drum of life you rarely thank.

Whisper this to yourself:

"My thoughts are not my truth.

My emotions are not my enemies.

My past is not my prison.

I am learning, healing, and returning to myself. One question at a time."

📌 **Chapter Summary:**

Emotions are not the enemy of logic.

They are the language of your deeper self.

Learn to listen, not obey. Learn to question, not suppress.

Learn to dance – not to fight – with your thoughts and feelings.

Chapter 3: Emotional Intelligence — The Superpower You Were Never Taught

"In a very real sense, we have two minds, one that thinks and one that feels." – Daniel Goleman

🔒 You Were Taught Math, But Not Meaning

You learnt how to multiply numbers.

You learnt how to write essays.

You memorised the capitals of countries you've never been to.

But did anyone ever teach you how to:

- Sit with your own shame without imploding?
- Apologise without ego?
- Speak your truth without collapsing in guilt?
- Recognise when you're projecting your pain onto someone else?

No. You were likely never taught **emotional intelligence** — and yet, it governs almost **every outcome in your life.**

Emotional intelligence isn't soft.

It's not optional.

It is the **operating system for everything else.**

Relationships. Leadership. Mental health. Communication. Parenting. Decision-making.

They all rise or fall on the foundation of how well you **understand and manage your emotions — and the emotions of others.**

Let's dive in.

🧠 3.1 What Is Emotional Intelligence, Really?

"It is very important to understand that emotional intelligence is not the opposite of intelligence; it is not the triumph of heart over head – it is the unique intersection of both." – David Caruso

We live in a world that celebrates **intellect** and **accomplishment.** From school grades to corporate promotions, we're rewarded for performance, analysis, and results.

But what happens when:

- A brilliant employee melts under pressure.
- A top student lashes out at criticism.
- A successful leader drives away talent with their ego.
- A parent reacts in rage before understanding a child's fear.

That's where intelligence **without emotional intelligence** collapses.

🔍 Emotional Intelligence (EI) Defined:

Emotional intelligence is the **ability to be aware of, understand, manage, and express one's emotions — while also being able to understand and influence the emotions of others.**

Let's break that down into human terms:

- You know what you're feeling and *why*.
- You don't explode or collapse under that feeling.
- You can stay present while someone else is feeling something big.
- You can communicate what you need without blaming or begging.

- You can detect subtle shifts in tone, body language, and energy.

This is not fluff. This is the **foundation of all human relationships** – with yourself and others.

🔁 3.2 Why Emotional Intelligence Is a Superpower

"When awareness is brought to emotion, power is brought to your life." – Tara Meyer Robson

Let's walk through **why EI is your greatest asset** – not just personally, but professionally and socially.

🧨 **Without EI, you may:**

- Destroy a relationship with one reactive sentence.
- Misinterpret someone's silence as rejection.
- Blow up a team with unresolved tension.
- Push away the very people trying to love you.
- Make decisions you regret but justify with logic.

We've all done it.

But EI helps you **pause**. And in that pause, you find your power.

You learn to:

- **De-escalate** your own reactivity.
- **Understand** the feelings behind someone's words.
- **Communicate** your needs clearly.
- **See people** instead of defending against them.
- **Respond**, rather than **react.**

🎯 **In Action:**

- A leader with EI builds trust, even in tough conversations.

- A teacher with EI notices the sadness behind a student's silence.
- A parent with EI validates a child's fear instead of punishing the expression of it.
- A partner with EI says, "Help me understand what you're feeling," instead of, "Why are you so emotional?"

This isn't "nice". It's **necessary.**

🧭 3.3 Self-Awareness – The First Gate

"Self-awareness doesn't stop you from making mistakes. It allows you to learn from them."

🔦 **Self-awareness is the superpower of:**

- Noticing your emotional state in real time
- Naming your emotion
- Understanding where it comes from
- Recognising the **pattern** or **trigger** it belongs to

🧠 **The Neuroscience:**

The more self-aware you are, the **more active your prefrontal cortex becomes** — the part of your brain that helps with reflection, planning, and emotional regulation. Less self-awareness = more amygdala hijack (fight/flight/freeze).

🔁 **Example:**

- You snap at your partner.
- You pause and ask, "Why did I react like that?"
- You realise it reminded you of being unheard as a child.
- Now, instead of defending the behaviour, you explore the **trigger beneath it.**

That is self-awareness in action.

✍ **Reflective Questions:**

- When I get reactive, what am I *feeling*?
- What emotional themes repeat in my life?
- What are my emotional blind spots?

Self-awareness is not guilt. It is **clarity**.

3.4 Self-Regulation – The Power of the Pause

"You don't have to attend every emotional argument you're invited to."

Self-regulation is not about *bottling up*.

It's about knowing how to:

- Pause
- Breathe
- Reflect
- Choose a **response** that aligns with who you want to be.

Scenario:

You're about to send a scathing email. You're furious.

But you pause. You sit with the anger. You realise it's rooted in feeling disrespected.

You rewrite the email with clarity and confidence — *not venom*.

That's not weakness. That's mastery.

Emotionally intelligent people don't deny emotions. They **choose** when and how to express them.

Real Tools:

- Breathing exercises (4-7-8 method)
- Body scans (where is the tension?)
- Journaling before reacting.

- Repeating: *"This is how I feel, not who I am."*

🔥 3.5 Motivation – Fuel That Lasts

"People with high EI are more motivated, even in the face of setbacks."

True motivation doesn't come from applause.

It comes from **alignment** – between values, purpose, and emotion.

🔄 Intrinsic Motivation Is EI in Motion:

- I don't work out to look good. I do it to feel strong.
- I don't study to impress. I do it to expand.
- I don't stay consistent to win approval. I do it because I believe in who I'm becoming.

Emotionally intelligent people **know their why** – and it keeps them moving even when the crowd is silent.

✍ Ask Yourself:

- What makes me feel *alive*?
- When do I feel most like myself?
- What would I do if no one clapped – but it still felt meaningful?

❤ 3.6 Empathy – The Skill That Heals

"Empathy is the highest form of knowledge." – Bill Bullard

Empathy is the ability to:

- Feel **with** someone, not for them.
- Sense their emotional state.
- Honour their experience – without judgement or projection.

💡 It's not:

- Fixing people

- Giving advice
- Dismissing feelings with "at least" statements
- Absorbing their emotions as your own

✅ **Empathy in Practice:**

- "That sounds hard. I'm here if you want to talk."
- "I don't know what to say, but I won't leave you alone in this."
- "What would support look like for you right now?"

Empathy doesn't always use words. Sometimes it's just **presence.**

🫶 3.7 Social Skills – The Mirror of Emotional Maturity

"Connection is why we're here. It gives purpose and meaning to our lives." – Brené Brown

This is where it all comes together: **your ability to navigate relationships.**

Emotionally Intelligent People:

- Listen without interrupting.
- Apologise without excuses.
- Give feedback without shaming.
- Set boundaries without guilt.
- Repair after rupture without ego

💬 **They use phrases like:**

- "Here's how I felt when that happened..."
- "Can we talk about what's not working – without blaming?"
- "That wasn't my intention, but I understand how it landed that way."
- "Thank you for being honest with me. I didn't realise that."

These are not scripts. They are signals – of safety, maturity, and respect.

Social skill isn't about charisma. It's about **emotional fluency** in connection.

3.8 Pause & Reflect .

"Emotional intelligence begins not with others, but within. To master it, you must first be willing to meet yourself in silence."

This isn't the part you skim.

This is the part where everything we've explored so far – **self-awareness, regulation, empathy, motivation, and connection** – becomes real, personal, and alive.

Take a moment before reading on.

Put down your phone.

Close the tabs in your mind.

Drop into your breath.

These next questions aren't here to entertain you.

They're here to **awaken you.**

1. What emotion do I struggle the most to acknowledge – and why?

Is it **anger**?

Were you taught that it's wrong to express it – that it's "ugly", "unspiritual", or "uncontrolled"?

Is it **sadness**?

Were you told to "be strong" or "move on" – before you ever had the chance to process what broke you?

Is it **joy**?

Do you feel guilty being happy while others struggle?

Many of us are **at war with parts of ourselves.**

Emotional intelligence begins when we **end the war** – by meeting every emotion with understanding, not judgement.

🔎 Reflect:

- Which emotion do I hide?
- Who taught me to hide it?
- What might change in my life if I let myself fully feel it – without shame?

🧊 2. When I feel emotionally overwhelmed, what do I usually do?

Do you **numb out** – with food, phones, scrolling, alcohol, or overworking?

Do you **explode** – lash out, yell, and blame?

Do you **implode** – go silent, withdraw, and self-blame?

Every response is a **strategy for survival.** But not all survival strategies are sustainable.

Emotional intelligence doesn't mean you never get overwhelmed.

It means you **notice it faster** and choose a healthier response.

🧠 Ask yourself:

- What's my emotional escape route?
- What would it look like to *stay* with the feeling – and listen to it?

🧭 3. What are my emotional blind spots – the parts I don't want to admit?

We all have them.

Maybe it's:

- A **need for validation** you mask as independence.

- A **fear of intimacy** you cover with sarcasm.
- A **control pattern** you hide behind logic.
- A **grudge** you spiritualise as "boundaries".

Emotional intelligence requires **radical self-honesty** – not to punish yourself, but to free yourself.

Mirror Moment:

- What part of me am I still trying to hide from the world?
- And what part of me am I still hiding from myself?

4. How often do I listen to understand... versus listening to defend or fix?

Think about your last few conversations.

Were you truly listening... Or were you:

- Preparing your comeback?
- Waiting to prove your point?
- Trying to fix the other person's feelings so *you* feel comfortable?

Empathy starts with **presence** – not problem-solving.

And emotional intelligence means **being with someone's feelings**, not just trying to change them.

Challenge:

- Practice listening without interrupting.
- Respond with: *"I hear you. Tell me more."*
- Notice what shifts when you stop trying to fix and start trying to understand.

🔥 5. What's one emotionally intelligent phrase I can start using today – in relationships, work, or parenting?

Let's equip you with **new language** – words that build connection instead of disconnection.

Here are a few emotionally intelligent phrases:

- "I'm not sure what you need, but I want to understand."
- "I felt hurt when that happened – can we talk about it?"
- "Can we press pause? I need a moment to respond, not react."
- "It's okay to feel this. You're safe here."
- "I was wrong – and I'm here to make it right."

✨ Choose one. Practice it. Use it in a conversation this week.

Watch how it changes the emotional tone of your interactions.

6. Who taught me how to feel? And what do I need to unlearn?

We don't just feel emotions. We **inherit emotional blueprints** from our families, cultures, and environments.

Ask yourself:

- Was I allowed to cry?
- Was vulnerability celebrated – or silenced?
- Did anyone model how to repair after conflict?

Emotional intelligence is often less about learning new things... and more about **unlearning the emotional limitations we were taught.**

✍ Journaling Prompt (Optional, but powerful):

"The emotion I've buried the longest is __________.

When I finally allowed myself to feel it, I noticed __________.

And now, I am learning that I can __________."

🍃 Final Reflection:

Take a breath.

You've just done something most people avoid their whole lives:

You've **faced your emotional truth**.

That is not weakness.

That is strength in its most evolved form.

This is how emotional intelligence is built – not in theory, but in moments like this...

...When you slow down long enough to hear the whisper underneath the chaos.

🧠 Final Thought:

Emotional intelligence is not about being calm all the time.

It's about knowing when to speak, when to pause, and when to feel fully without letting the feeling run the show.

Chapter 4: Say It with Soul

"I've come to the frightening conclusion that I am the decisive element in the classroom. It is my personal approach that creates the climate." - Dr Haim Ginott

🌑 What If the Way You Speak... Shapes the Way Others Heal?

Imagine a world where people feel safe in your presence.

Your words don't just deliver information — they deliver ***dignity***.

Where conversations don't destroy confidence — they restore it.

Where language becomes a bridge, not a blade.

That's not a fantasy. That's empathic communication.

That's the world of Dr Haim Ginott — the quiet revolutionary of compassionate speech.

Most people don't know his name.

But millions have been transformed by his philosophy:

"People may not remember what you said, but they will never forget how you made them feel — especially when they were vulnerable."

🌑 4.1 What If the Way You Speak Shapes the Way Others Heal?

"Every word you speak is either a bridge... or a barrier."

We don't just communicate with facts. We communicate with **tone, timing, intention**, and — most of all — **emotional energy**.

You might not remember what someone said to you 10 years ago.

But you remember **how it made you feel.**

That teacher who made you feel brilliant.

That parent who crushed you with one sentence.

That partner who comforted you with just a wordless glance.

Why? Because **communication is not about information – it's about transformation.**

The way we speak can:

- Calm a nervous system.
- Trigger a trauma response.
- Inspire action.
- Erode trust.
- Create intimacy.
- Or widen the emotional distance.

So, let's stop seeing conversations as mere exchanges of data – and start seeing them as **sacred spaces.**

👶 4.2 Who Was Dr Haim Ginott?

Though we've removed his name from the chapter title, **his spirit runs through every word.**

Dr Haim Ginott was a pioneer who understood something that many miss:

The tone you set – especially with vulnerable minds – becomes the inner voice they carry for life.

He saw how words spoken to children shaped:

- Their self-worth
- Their emotional expression
- Their resilience
- Their trust in others
- Their inner narratives

And what he learnt applies to all relationships – not just with children. Whether you're leading a team, mentoring a student, managing conflict, or comforting a friend – the same rules apply:

Validate the emotion.

Set limits on the behaviour.

Speak to the experience, not just the outcome.

It's timeless wisdom for any soul who seeks to **communicate with compassion.**

💣 4.3 The Power of Words – More Than Language, It's Energy

"Words are not just tools. They are keys. Or they are weapons."

Words can either:

- **Open someone's heart** or shut it down.
- **Light up someone's self-worth** or plunge it into darkness.
- **Validate pain** or deepen it.

We must understand that **language is more than grammar**. It's energetic.

And the energy behind your words is what people remember.

🔥 Real-Life Echoes of Words:

- *"You always mess this up."* → becomes a child's inner critic.
- *"You're such a drama queen."* → becomes an adult's emotional shame.
- *"You're so lazy."* → becomes someone's struggle with worthiness.
- *"You're amazing just as you are."* → becomes a person's grounding truth.

Think of your words as **emotional tattoos**. They don't wash off easily.

So, when you speak – ask yourself:

"Will this phrase linger as healing... or harm?"

🧭 4.4 The Golden Rule of Compassionate Speech

"Never deny the emotion. Deny the behaviour if needed – but validate the feeling first."

This single principle is *life-altering*. Why?

Because we live in a culture that shames emotion.

People are told:

- "Calm down."
- "You're overreacting."
- "Don't be so emotional."
- "Man up."
- "Stop being dramatic."

These aren't just dismissals. They're emotional shutdown commands.

🧠 Here's what happens neurologically:

- When a person's emotion is dismissed, their **limbic system** (emotional centre) goes into defence mode.
- No learning. No growth. Just **fight, flight, or freeze.**

But when you **validate a feeling**, the nervous system calms.

The person feels seen. The brain is now ready to engage.

🔁 **Transformation Example:**

Instead of: "Stop whining. It's just homework."

Say: "It feels hard right now, doesn't it? Want to take a break and come back together?"

Instead of "Why are you being so sensitive?"

Say: "That really affected you. I want to understand why."

One uses shame.

The other uses a soul.

🛠 4.5 Tools & Techniques for Soulful Communication

This is where *Say It with Soul* becomes a practice – not just a philosophy.

Let's get practical.

🧠 1. Acknowledge Emotion Before Anything Else

Wrong: "You need to fix this."

Right: "This must feel overwhelming. Let's figure it out together."

💡 Why it works: You create emotional safety first – then discuss solutions.

🔄 2. Use Reflective Listening

"So, what I'm hearing is... you felt left out when I didn't include you."

This technique builds **clarity, trust, and empathy** – and helps the speaker feel heard *without* you needing to fix or rescue.

🛑 3. Avoid Minimisers

Phrases like:

- "At least..."
- "It's not that bad..."
- "Others have it worse..."

Sound comforting, but they **dismiss emotional reality.**

✨ Instead, say:

"That sounds heavy. I don't have answers, but I'm with you in this."

💬 4. Create Emotional Permission

Sometimes people don't open up because they feel like they *shouldn't* feel what they're feeling.

Say things like:

- "It's okay to cry."
- "You're allowed to be mad."
- "This would shake anyone. You don't have to hide it."

You are giving someone **psychological permission to be human.**

🔥 5. Say What Heals

Some phrases carry generational healing:

- "I see you."
- "You matter to me."
- "That makes sense."
- "I'm not going anywhere."
- "You're allowed to feel this."
- "That was wrong – and it wasn't your fault."
- "You don't have to explain it all. I believe you."

This is **emotional alchemy**.

Your words = their transformation.

🔄 4.6 The Repair Principle – You Can Always Try Again

"Emotional intelligence isn't about being perfect – it's about knowing how to repair."

We all say the wrong thing.

We all react instead of responding.

We all raise our voices when we mean to raise safety.

And that's okay – **if you know how to repair.**

💬 **The 4 Steps to Repair:**

1. **Acknowledge:** "I messed up."
2. **Validate:** "I can see how that hurt you."
3. **Own:** "That's on me – not you."
4. **Reconnect:** "Can we rebuild this together?"

No ego. No excuses. Just emotional maturity.

People don't need you to be flawless.

They need you to be **accountable, emotionally aware, and safe.**

🖤 4.7 Everyday Application: Parenting, Teaching, Leading, Loving

As a parent:

- "I love you even when you're upset."
- "You can tell me anything – even the hard stuff."

As a teacher:

- "I noticed you were quiet today. That's okay. I'm here if you want to talk."
- "Your effort matters to me more than your score."

As a partner:

- "I felt distant between us yesterday. Can we talk about what was going on?"
- "You don't have to hide your feelings from me. I want all of you."

As a leader:

- "You don't have to be perfect here. Just real."

- "Let's talk about what's not working – and make it better together."

In any role, your words carry weight.

Use them with wisdom.

Speak from the soul, not from fear.

4.8 Pause & Reflect (Deep Version)

Let's slow down.

Ask yourself:

- When I'm emotionally uncomfortable, do I listen or shut down?
- What phrases do I repeat that might be harming those I love – without realising it?
- What did I need to hear as a child... that I can start saying to others now?

Write them down. Use them. Start speaking the words **you once craved.**

You'll be surprised how they heal you too.

Chapter Summary (Soul-Level)

Communication is not a tool. It is a sacred space.

The words you speak shape nervous systems, beliefs, and identities.

Every sentence is a choice: harm or healing. Blame or belonging. Shame or safety.

Speak with soul.

And you'll become the kind of presence that people feel safe remembering.

Chapter 5: The Power of Mindset — Embracing Growth

"Your beliefs become your thoughts, your thoughts become your words, your words become your actions, your actions become your habits, your habits become your values, and your values become your destiny."

– Mahatma Gandhi

💥 Your Mindset Is Either Your Freedom... or Your Prison

Let's not waste time sugarcoating it.

Right now, as you read this, you are either:

- Growing
- Or defending the reasons why you're not.

There is no neutral ground.

Every excuse, every avoidance, every "I'm just like this" you tell yourself...

is a lock on the prison door of your potential.

You were not born to play small. You were conditioned to believe you had to.

This chapter?

It's not a motivational speech. It's a **mental rebellion.**

It's a **breakup letter to your limiting beliefs.**

Let's start by naming your enemy.

5.1 Your Mindset Is Either Your Freedom... or Your Prison

"The chains you wear are the stories you tell yourself about who you are."

Every day, you live inside a world shaped by your mind – not your circumstances.

The same situation could break one person and build another. Why?

Not because one is stronger – but because one believes in the possibility of growth, and the other believes in the permanence of pain.

Your mindset is not just a filter.

It's a **foundational force** that shapes:

- What you try
- What you avoid
- How you respond to failure
- How you process feedback
- Whether you shrink or stretch

You either believe:

"This is happening *to* me."

or

"This is happening *for* me – so I can evolve."

And that one shift? Changes everything.

🔥 **Quote Break:**

"You can't have a million-dollar dream with a minimum-wage mindset."

– Stephen C. Hogan

"The greatest prison people live in is the fear of what others think."

– David Icke

🧱 5.2 Fixed Mindset: The Silent Killer of Potential

"People with a fixed mindset believe that effort is a sign of inadequacy. People with a growth mindset believe effort is how you build greatness."

A fixed mindset doesn't show up as a loud voice.

It's sneaky. Whispering things like:

- "If I were really smart, this would be easy."
- "I'm just not good at public speaking."
- "I'm not creative like them."
- "People like me don't succeed."
- "If I fail, I'll look stupid."
- "If I try and fail, I'll prove I'm not enough."

It sounds logical. But underneath it?

It's just **fear disguised as intelligence.**

💣 **The Cost of a Fixed Mindset:**

- You avoid challenges.
- You play small to protect ego.
- You choose being right over being real.
- You seek approval instead of mastery.
- You settle – and call it peace.

"Better safe than sorry" is the anthem of the stuck.

But make no mistake:

A fixed mindset doesn't just sabotage your future. It kills your aliveness.

🌱 5.3 Growth Mindset: The Ruthless Rebirth

"The mind is everything. What you think, you become."

– Buddha

A **growth mindset** is not positive thinking.

It's **warrior thinking.**

It says:

- "I'm willing to suck before I get good."
- "I'll outlearn every limitation placed on me."
- "My past is not a prophecy. It's a lesson."
- "Feedback is not an attack – it's a tool."
- "I don't fear failure – I fear *never trying*."

A growth mindset doesn't coddle your ego.

It challenges it – and **refuses to let you stay small.**

🌊 Real-Life Shift:

Old You: *"I failed – that means I'm not cut out for this."*

New You: *"I failed – that means I'm *in the game* and *growing strength."*

Old You: *"I'm not naturally good at this."*

New You: *"Then I'm going to become someone who is."*

🔥 Quote Drop:

"Success is not final. Failure is not fatal. It is the courage to continue that counts."

– Winston Churchill

"In a growth mindset, failure is not evidence of unintelligence. It is a heartening springboard for growth."

– Carol Dweck

🔍 5.4 What's REALLY Holding You Back?

"Most people aren't afraid of failure. They're afraid of being seen as a failure."

Let's call it out.

You're not lazy. You're not unmotivated.

You're afraid that **if you change, people won't love you anymore.**

You're afraid of:

- Outgrowing your circle
- Succeeding and feeling alone
- Becoming someone who threatens the comfort of others.
- Disappointing the version of yourself others feel safe around.

But listen:

Growth will cost you people who only loved the version of you that didn't love yourself.

Still worth it?

Yes. Every. Single. Time.

Because of the person you're becoming?

That's someone *you* will finally respect.

5.5 Neuroplasticity – You Are Meant to Change

"You are not stuck. You are just attached to patterns that feel safe."

Neuroplasticity says your brain is **not fixed.**

Every experience you engage in, every belief you challenge, every skill you practise – is literally **rewiring your neurones.**

This means:

- You can stop overthinking.
- You can unlearn shame.
- You can build discipline.
- You can become confident.
- You can transform your identity.

It doesn't happen overnight.

It happens through **consistent disruption of the old story.**

💥 **Truth Bomb:**

Your brain doesn't care if the belief is true. It only cares if it's familiar. If you want to change your life, make truth feel more familiar than fear.

🧨 5.6 Stop Calling It "Just Who I Am".

"The most dangerous phrase in your vocabulary is 'That's just the way I am.'"

It sounds innocent.

It's a death sentence for growth.

You say:

- "I've always been shy."
- "I'm not a morning person."
- "I'm just bad with money."
- "I don't do confrontation."
- "I'm not the confident type."

But what you're really saying is:

"I've decided to protect my limitations more than my potential."

No one is born confident. Or productive. Or resilient.

They become that way by **deciding that their pain doesn't get the final word.**

🔥 **Reframe:**

Instead of: *"That's just how I am."*

Say, *"That's how I've been – until now."*

5.7 The Most Dangerous Mindset in the World: Apathy

"The opposite of love isn't hate. It's indifference." – Elie Wiesel

Apathy is the mindset of:

- "Why bother?"

- "Nothing ever changes."
- "This is just life."
- "It is what it is."

It feels safe. But it's a **slow emotional death**.

You stop trying.

You stop feeling.

You stop caring – not because you're at peace... but because hope feels dangerous.

But apathy is not peace.

It is **unresolved pain wearing a mask.**

The cure?

Do something different – even if it scares the hell out of you.

🧘 5.8 Ruthless Self-Awareness: Audit Your Mind

This isn't self-help fluff. This is **psychological honesty**.

Ask yourself:

- Who benefits from me playing small?
- What belief about myself am I still treating like law?
- Where am I hiding behind comfort and calling it "balance"?
- What identity do I need to bury to birth a stronger one?

Write. Reflect. Rage if you must.

Then rise.

✍ Reflection Journal Prompt:

"The story I've been telling myself about my limits is: ____________.

Today, I choose to outgrow that story – and replace it with: ____________."

Repeat it. Embody it. Make it your truth.

📌 Chapter Summary – Say Goodbye to Your Old Mindset

This isn't about motivation.

This is about **transformation.**

If you want to change your life, you must:

- Kill the lies.
- Rewire the beliefs.
- Stretch through the fear.
- Fall in love with the messy, glorious process of **becoming.**

"The future belongs to those who believe in the beauty of their own rewiring."

– Eleanor Roosevelt

Chapter 6: Transform to Transcend — Real Stories of Behavioural Breakthroughs

"Change happens when the pain of staying the same becomes greater than the pain of transformation."

– Tony Robbins

🌱 What Makes a Transformation Real?

It's not the books you read.

Not the quotes you post.

Not the workshops you attend.

Real transformation happens in moments that crack you open:

- When your identity breaks
- When your patterns backfire
- When your inner child screams for something better
- When you finally say, "I can't live like this anymore."

In this chapter, you're going to meet **real people** who stepped into that fire – and didn't just survive...

They rebuilt from the ashes.

Each story here is personal.

Each one speaks not just to the brain – but to the *soul.*

🧠 Case Study 1: Rahul – From Self-Doubt to Quiet Strength

"I used to shrink so others wouldn't feel small around me."

– Rahul, 31, Product Designer, Bangalore

🔍 Background:

Rahul had a brilliant mind. Sharp eye for detail. Deep empathy.

But every time he spoke up in meetings, he doubted himself.

Every time he pitched an idea, he prefaced it with:

"This might be stupid, but..."

He was drowning in **invisible self-rejection.**

He told himself:

- "I'm not a natural leader."
- "People like me don't rise."
- "Better stay quiet than be wrong."

Where did it come from?

🧸 The Origin:

As a child, Rahul had a hypercritical father.

Praise was rare.

Correction was constant.

The unspoken rule was: *Don't make mistakes – or you'll be made to feel stupid.*

So, Rahul built an identity around **emotional safety** through silence.

He became *"the quiet one"*.

But inside, he had a voice begging to be heard.

🔄 The Shift:

Rahul's manager one day said:

"You have ideas worth hearing. The only person silencing you... is you."

That night, Rahul sat down and wrote **every time he had stayed silent** out of fear.

It hit him: his life wasn't being shaped by talent – it was being shaped by **a belief that he didn't belong.**

⚡ **Action Taken:**

- He began therapy.
- He stopped prefacing his ideas with apologies.
- He took up improv classes to challenge his fear of judgement.
- He started a Medium blog to reclaim his voice.

💥 **Result:**

6 months later, Rahul presented a redesign to a board of investors – and they approved funding for an entirely new product line.

He didn't just find his voice.

He **reclaimed his right to take space** in the room.

🧠 **Anecdote 1: Nina – The Girl Who Cried... Then Led**

"My strength didn't come from hiding emotion. It came from owning it."

– Nina, 25, Startup Founder, Pune

Nina used to cry in meetings.

Not because she was weak – but because she **cared**. Because she **felt deeply.**

But in her world – the male-dominated tech startup space – emotion was weakness.

So, she started muting herself.

Toughening up. Hardening.

Until one day, after her team missed a funding deadline, she exploded.

Tears. Rage. Shame.

And instead of apologising, she stood up and said:

"This is what leadership looks like when it's real. Not polished. Not perfect. But present."

From that day, her team respected her more – not less.

She didn't stop being emotional.

She just stopped **apologising** for being **human.**

Case Study 2: Aryan – From Rage to Reflection

"They called me aggressive. I was just unparented."

– Aryan, 34, Sales Manager, Delhi

Aryan had always been the loud one.

Commanding. Charming. But also, *explosive.*

He prided himself on being "brutally honest".

But honesty without empathy? That's just **emotional laziness.**

His relationships were falling apart.

Colleagues feared him.

His wife once said, "You win every argument – and lose everyone you love."

That broke him.

The Inner Wound:

Aryan grew up in chaos.

Emotion was survival.

He had no emotional vocabulary – only **rage, silence, or sarcasm.**

Underneath the aggression?

A terrified little boy, constantly bracing for abandonment.

The Turning Point:

In therapy, he was asked:

"When was the first time you realised anger got you attention?"

He wept. For the first time in 15 years.

Growth Actions:

- He began practising nonviolent communication.
- Started journaling every emotional reaction.
- Read Dr Gabor Maté's *When the Body Says No*
- Repaired key relationships with raw, honest apologies.

Outcome:

Aryan didn't lose his fire – he **learnt to focus it.**

Now, he leads with impact – not intimidation.

And his team says they've "never felt more emotionally safe around a leader".

Anecdote 2: Leah – The Quietest in Class, Now Loud in Life

"They called me invisible. I became inevitable."

– Leah, 19, Student, Hyderabad

Leah barely spoke in school.

Not because she had nothing to say – but because **no one ever really listened.**

She felt like a shadow in her own life.

Until one poetry competition changed everything.

She stood on stage, voice shaking, heart pounding.

And shared a piece called *"If I Stay Silent, I'll Die Slowly"*.

By the time she was done, there was not a dry eye in the room.

That moment? It shattered her silence.

Now, she's:

- President of her college's spoken word club
- Started a nonprofit teaching poetry to underprivileged girls.
- Studying psychology to become the person *she once needed*

🧠 Case Study 3: Ishaan & Tara – A Marriage Saved by Emotional Intelligence

"We didn't fall out of love. We just stopped speaking the language of empathy."

– Ishaan, 40, Entrepreneur

Ishaan and Tara were two high-achieving individuals... with a marriage on life support.

Arguments were frequent.

Misunderstandings daily.

Both felt unheard, unseen, and **unloved**.

They tried therapy. It didn't "work".

Until one session, the therapist said:

"You don't need solutions. You need emotional safety."

That was the game-changer.

🧠 The Shift:

- They read Dr Sue Johnson's *Hold Me Tight* together.
- Learnt to **reflect** instead of react.
- Started practising **"mirroring"** (repeating what the other said before replying)
- Used "I feel..." instead of "You always..."

💬 **Transformation Dialogue:**

Before:

"You don't care about me!"

"You're always working!"

After:

"I feel neglected when you miss dinner. It makes me feel unimportant."

"I'm sorry. I didn't realise work was making you feel abandoned."

Today, they're stronger than ever.

Not because their issues vanished –

but because they **learnt to speak soul-to-soul**, not ego-to-ego.

🧘 **Pause & Reflect: Which One of These Stories Was *Yours* in Disguise?**

- Do you silence your voice like Rahul?
- Do you numb emotion like Aryan once did?
- Do you wear perfection like armour, like Nina?
- Do you crave safety but sabotage connection like Ishaan?
- Do you hide your power like Leah did?

Transformation starts with **honesty.**

Then, it demands **action.**

📌 **Chapter Summary:**

Transformation is not always loud.

Sometimes, it begins in a whisper: *"Enough."*

Real change doesn't come from books or lectures.

It comes from:

- Owning your wounds

- Questioning your patterns
- Speaking your truth
- Choosing to evolve – even when it's uncomfortable.

Each story in this chapter?

Was once a person who believed they couldn't change.

And yet, here they are.

Rewritten.

Reclaimed.

Risen.

📝 Reflection Workbook: Rewriting Your Own Narrative (Transform to Transcend)

"Sometimes the most powerful thing you can do is stop, turn inward, and ask yourself, 'What have I been pretending not to know?"

✍ Section 1: Mirror Moments – What Did These Stories Reflect Back to You?

Take your time. There is no rush. These questions are designed to stir your subconscious, unlock buried stories, and help you begin writing **a new emotional identity.**

🔍 1. Which person's story in Chapter 6 did you relate to most – and why?

- What part of their emotional journey mirrored your own?
- What emotions did it bring up for you?
- Have you ever silenced, sabotaged, or suppressed yourself in a similar way?

_ "When I read about ____________, I felt ___________, *because..."*

"Their journey reminded me of the time when I..."

🔎 **2. What recurring emotional pattern are you tired of repeating?**

- Overthinking?
- Shutting down?
- Angry outbursts?
- Fear of judgement?
- Fear of intimacy or vulnerability?

Now go deeper: where do you believe that pattern **originated**?

_ "The pattern I keep repeating is __________."

_ "I believe it began when __________."

🔎 **3. What belief about yourself is no longer serving you — but still lives in you?**

- "I'm not good enough."
- "I can't trust people."
- "I'm not meant for success."
- "I'm hard to love."
- "If I speak my truth, I'll be rejected."

Let's confront it.

_ "The old belief that still runs my life is _________."

_ "I know this belief is not true because _________."

🔁 **Section 2: Shift the Script — From Reaction to Rewriting**

Now that you've faced your patterns, let's start **rewriting the inner code.**

🔧 **4. Create a new belief to replace the old one:**

_ "The belief I am choosing now is: _________."

_ "When I live from this belief, I will feel _________."

🗣 5. What are 3 phrases you will start saying to yourself – with intention?

These should be emotionally honest, empowering, and personal. For example:

- "I am allowed to take up space."
- "Mistakes don't make me less worthy."
- "I will not shrink to soothe someone else's ego."
- "My past taught me – but it doesn't define me."

"My new affirmations are..."

💡 6. What "micro-change" will you implement in the next 24 hours?

Start small. Real transformation lives in consistency, not grand gestures.

Some ideas:

- Speak up in a meeting!
- Send the apology you've avoided.
- Journal through your next trigger.
- Say "I love you" to yourself aloud.
- Sit with discomfort instead of numbing it.

"The action I will take in the next 24 hours is __________ because I am ready to shift."

🌊 Section 3: Emotional Reset Ritual

When things get heavy – and they will – come back to this grounding prompt.

💬 Write a letter to your future self, who has already done the work.

Start with:

"Dear Future, Me, I know how hard it was to begin..."

Tell them:

- What you're scared of
- What you're letting go
- What you're stepping into
- How proud you are for not quitting.
- That you're still here – and still evolving.

Close the Reflection with This Commitment

"I am no longer the person I was.

I am not yet the person I will be.

But I am choosing to heal, one brave decision at a time.

This is no longer theory – this is my transformation in motion."

Sign it. Date it. Frame it.

Chapter 7: The Ripple Effects — Impact on Relationships and Community

"Your healing doesn't just change your life. It changes every life you touch from this point forward."

~ Anonymous

🔥 The Personal Is Always Political, Relational, and Generational

You thought healing was just about *you?*

You thought mindset was just about reaching your goals?

You thought regulating your emotions was for **your peace** alone?

Wrong.

When you grow, you **shift every room you walk into.**

When you break a toxic pattern, you end **a legacy of emotional inheritance.**

When you choose self-awareness, you choose to **raise the vibration of every conversation, relationship, and decision** around you.

"You don't heal in isolation. You heal in relationships. And then those relationships become healed because of you."

This chapter is not about becoming perfect — it's about becoming **a force of conscious energy** in a world addicted to emotional autopilot.

Let's explore every ripple — from your relationships to your community to your legacy.

7.1 Your Mindset Affects Everyone You Meet

"Your nervous system becomes part of the emotional ecosystem of those around you."

Ever walked into a room and **felt** the tension – even before a word was spoken?

That's not energy magic. That's emotional *contagion.*

Humans are wired for emotional resonance. Our brains have **mirror neurones** – which means:

- If you are anxious, others feel anxious.
- If you are grounded, others feel safe.
- If you are defensive, others tense up.
- If you are present, others soften.

Your **inner world** is always broadcasting signals to the **external world.**

So if you change *your inner software*, the system around you starts to **update itself.**

Real Talk:

- Your kids don't copy your advice. They copy your *emotional regulation.*
- Your team doesn't just hear your strategy. They *absorb your tone.*
- Your partner doesn't react to your words. They react to your *energy.*

You are a **living, breathing emotional blueprint.**

What are you broadcasting?

7.2 Healing in Relationships: The Brave Work of Relearning Connection

"Most of us don't need better communication. We need deeper emotional safety."

You cannot talk someone into trust.

You cannot fix a relationship with logic alone.

Because people don't just respond to your intellect – they respond to **how emotionally safe they feel with you.**

🧨 **Common Unconscious Patterns We Bring into Relationships:**

- The Pleaser: "If I keep everyone happy, I won't be rejected."
- The Avoider: "If I don't get too close, I won't get hurt."
- The Controller: "If I can manage every variable, I'll feel safe."
- The Performer: "If I'm successful enough, I'll finally be loved."
- The Fixer: "If I help them, maybe they'll stay."

These are not flaws. They're **survival styles** – formed long before we had a choice.

But at some point, you must ask:

"Is this version of me *still serving my relationships* – or just protecting my wounds?"

🌿 **Healing Looks Like:**

- Saying, "I need time to process," instead of stonewalling
- Saying, "I feel unsafe right now, but I want to stay present," instead of lashing out
- Apologising without explaining your trauma as a justification
- Letting others hold their pain without rescuing or fixing.
- Learning that *love doesn't mean abandoning yourself.*

🧘 **Pause & Practice:**

Journal Prompt:

_ "The relationship I most want to transform is _____________.

The pattern I keep repeating is _____________.

I learnt that from _____________.

What I choose now instead is ____________."

👨‍👩‍👧 7.3 Generational Ripple: When You Heal, You Break the Chain

"What you don't repair, you repeat. And what you repeat, you pass on."

Let's get brutally honest.

So many of us are still carrying:

- Our mother's fear.
- Our father's rage.
- Our culture's silence
- Our religion's shame
- Our society's performance mask

We were taught that emotions were a **liability**, not a language.

That survival meant shutting up, showing up, and staying small.

But you?

You're reading this chapter because **you are the pattern breaker.**

🧪 **Real Example:**

Tanya, 42, used to scream at her daughter the same way her mother screamed at her.

Every time, she felt regret. But also, shame.

Until one day, her daughter looked at her with teary eyes and said:

"You sound like Grandma. I thought you said you didn't want to be like her."

That broke her.

But it also *rebuilt* her.

She began:

- Reading books on conscious parenting
- Sitting with her shame instead of projecting it
- Owning her past without making it an excuse

And now, her daughter says:

"Mom still gets mad. But now, she listens. She asks me how I feel. I feel safer."

That's legacy.

That's generational change.

That's the ripple.

🧠 7.4 The Workplace Ripple: Leading with Emotional Authority

"Culture is not built by perks. It's built by presence."

Leaders who lack emotional intelligence:

- Create fear-based productivity.
- Avoid hard conversations.
- Blur the line between personal wounds and professional roles.
- Reward performance, punish vulnerability.

Leaders who are emotionally attuned:

- Create safe feedback loops.
- Address conflict early and compassionately.

- Know how to apologise without ego.
- Inspire loyalty – not fear.

💼 The Tools of an Emotionally Intelligent Leader:

- "Let's pause this meeting – I sense something deeper needs to be addressed."
- "I want to understand your experience, not just your results."
- "What do you need from me to feel more supported?"
- "Let's repair this, not just fix it."

When a leader gets emotionally healthy, **the whole team evolves.**

🧠 7.5 The Community Ripple: Your Growth Elevates the Collective

"One emotionally intelligent person in a group is enough to elevate the emotional tone of the room."

You don't need to be a celebrity to influence lives.

You don't need millions of followers to spark a movement.

You just need:

- A grounded nervous system
- A regulated voice
- A consistent alignment with your truth

You could be:

- The friend who doesn't gossip – and shifts the energy.
- The sibling who stops repeating family drama – and starts modelling peace.
- The stranger who validates someone's pain in an elevator – and changes their entire day.

This isn't about becoming a guru.

It's about becoming **a lighthouse** in a stormy world.

And you don't have to say a word.

Your presence is the ripple.

🧘 7.6 Pause & Reflect – How Are You Rippling Outward?

Use these prompts to see where your growth is already creating quiet revolutions:

- Who feels emotionally safer because of how you've evolved?
- What unconscious behaviour have you interrupted – that your younger self thought was normal?
- What space have you entered lately and elevated – just by being more self-aware?
- What words do you now *refuse* to speak because you've learnt better?

Write them down. Don't diminish them.

Every healed moment you choose creates **a future someone else gets to live in.**

🧠 7.7 You Are the Ecosystem Now

"When the flower doesn't bloom, you don't blame the flower. You change the soil."

You've changed your soil.

And now, you *are* the soil.

You are the safe space.

You are the emotional anchor.

You are the one who says, "It stops with me."

You are the evidence that transformation is real.

📌 Chapter Summary — You Are the Ripple

Your mindset shapes more than your mood.

Your healing shapes more than your habits.

It shapes your:

- Relationships
- Children
- Teams
- Culture
- Community
- World

You are not just healing for you.

You are healing for every person who will one day feel safe in your presence.

And that?

That is **power beyond performance.**

That is legacy.

📔 Ripple Journal Worksheet

Companion to Chapter 7: The Ripple Effects

"Every time you choose healing over reaction, awareness over autopilot, connection over control – you ripple. You shift the emotional climate around you. That's legacy."

~ Anonymous

🌱 Section 1: The First Ripple — You

1. How have you emotionally changed in the past year?

- Are you more patient?
- More honest?

- More emotionally expressive?
- Less reactive?
- Do you now pause before responding?

✏️ *Journal Response:*

"One shift I notice in how I feel, think, or respond is..."

2. What belief about yourself have you begun to question or dismantle?

✏️ *Write it out:*

_ "The old belief was: ______________________________"

_ "Now, I am starting to believe: ______________________________"

3. What personal habit or pattern are you no longer willing to tolerate in yourself?

This could be procrastination, defensiveness, silence during conflict, avoiding hard conversations, people-pleasing, etc.

✏️ *Your declaration:*

"I am done with ______________________ because I deserve better."

👥 Section 2: The Second Ripple – Your Relationships

4. Who in your life feels the impact of your inner work the most?

- A child?
- Your partner?
- A sibling?
- A colleague?
- Yourself?

✏ *Reflect:*

"_________ now feels safer, more seen, or more connected to me because I..." _

5. What conversation did you handle differently recently — and how did that change the outcome?

✏ *Story Prompt:*

_ "In the past, I would have ________________. But this time, I chose to _____________. *And as a result...*"

6. Where are you still reactive, and what does that reaction protect?

Anger? Deflection? Withdrawal? Sarcasm?

✏ *Write from awareness:*

_ "When I react with __________, it's usually protecting my fear of _________."

● Section 3: The Third Ripple — Your Community & Culture

7. How have you brought emotional intelligence into your workplace, school, family, or friend circle?

- Did you shift a toxic dynamic?
- Hold space for someone's vulnerability?
- Say what no one else would?
- Model emotional maturity.

✏ *Your ripple:*

_ "The space where I led with emotional presence instead of performance was _________."

8. What generational behaviour or belief are you interrupting in your family?

Name the chain-break:

_ "In my family, __________ was normalised. I no longer accept that as my truth. I'm replacing it with _________".

Section 4: Legacy in Motion

9. What does "emotional legacy" mean to you?

Define it in your own language:

"To me, emotional legacy means..."

10. What's one decision you've made lately that your *future self*— or future generation — will thank you for?

Affirm the ripple:

_ "Because I chose to __________ instead of _________, *my future will now..."*

Final Reflection:

Close your eyes. Place your hand on your heart.

Now write this like a commitment, a declaration, or even a prayer:

"I am no longer healing in silence.

I am rippling outward – into my relationships, my community, and my legacy.

My growth is not just about me.

It is about every soul I meet who will feel safer, lighter, freer...

because I chose to evolve."

Signed: ___________________________

Date: ___________________________

Chapter 8: The Anatomy of Emotional Triggers — Decoding Your Reaction Patterns

"You will keep being triggered until you heal the wound. Pain is a teacher. Your nervous system is your syllabus."

~ Anonymous

🔥 Section 8.1: What Is a Trigger, Really?

Let's get brutally honest — most people walk around like emotional landmines. Smiling on the outside, screaming inside. All it takes is **a word, a look, a pause too long**, and boom — they explode.

But what is that explosion?

A **trigger** is not the event. It's **your body remembering a time you didn't feel safe** and reacting to protect you — even if the threat no longer exists.

It's when your adult self is in the room, but your 9-year-old self takes over the wheel.

Triggers are evidence of **unresolved emotional memory**.

They show up when:

- Your boss gives you feedback, and it feels like being scolded by a parent.
- Your partner goes silent, and it reminds you of being emotionally abandoned.
- A friend cancels plans, and you spiral into "they don't care."

"A trigger is the past banging on the door of the present, demanding to be healed."

🍬 Section 8.2: The Anatomy of a Trigger – What Happens Inside You?

When you're triggered, it's not just psychological – it's **neurological.** Your entire system **goes into survival mode.**

Let's break it down:

1. The Spark: A Moment Happens

It can be as subtle as a facial expression or as explicit as someone yelling. To others, it's no big deal. To you, it's *danger.*

2. The Brain Lights Up

The amygdala (your fear centre) hijacks your reasoning brain. You're no longer **thinking logically** – you're **reliving emotionally.**

3. The Nervous System Reacts

You might:

- Freeze (shut down, go numb)
- Flight (withdraw, avoid)
- Fight (get defensive or lash out)
- Fawn (people-please to feel safe)

Your heartbeat quickens. Muscles tense. Cortisol floods your bloodstream. You're not in a conversation – **you're in a battlefield.**

4. The Story Machine Activates

Your brain makes up a fast story:

- "They don't love me."
- "I'm about to be abandoned."
- "I'm not enough."

- "They're trying to control me."

This story isn't about *now*. It's a flashback – an echo of a wound your inner child still carries.

"Triggers are not weaknesses. They are maps. Every reaction is a clue to what still needs healing."

🎭 Section 8.3: The Hidden Faces of Triggers – The 5 Archetypes

Triggers wear different masks – depending on your story.

🔥 The Rejection Trigger

Surface Story: "They ignored me."

Core Wound: "I'm not loveable unless I'm perfect."

🔥 The Abandonment Trigger

Surface Story: "They didn't choose me."

Core Wound: "People always leave me."

🔥 The Control Trigger

Surface Story: "Stop telling me what to do!"

Core Wound: "I had no power as a child."

🔥 The Shame Trigger

Surface Story: "They're judging me."

Core Wound: "I am not enough. I am defective."

🔥 The Neglect Trigger

Surface Story: "You didn't even notice me."

Core Wound: "I only matter when I overgive."

Each of these archetypes represents an **unmet emotional need**. And unless we learn to meet those needs consciously, they keep hijacking our behaviour.

🧒 Section 8.4: Meet Your Inner Child – The One Really Feeling the Trigger

Imagine this:

Your boss says, "This presentation could be better."

You smile and nod.

But inside, your chest tightens, and tears pool behind your eyes.

Why?

Because the 10-year-old version of you – who once got told "you're a disappointment" – just took over.

The adult, you aren't in pain.

Your inner child is.

And until you learn to **parent that child**, you'll keep reacting from pain instead of responding from power.

"Behind every adult meltdown is a child who needs or once needed comfort – not criticism."

🛠 Section 8.5: How to Work Through a Trigger – The Conscious Response Method™

This method takes just **90 seconds** – but it can save relationships, jobs, and sanity.

🧘 1. Pause

Don't speak. Don't act. Just notice.

"I'm feeling a surge of emotion. This is a trigger."

2. Breathe

3 deep breaths to **signal safety** to your nervous system.

3. Name It

Say it aloud or write it:

"I feel... rejected, hurt, overwhelmed."

Naming your emotion activates your prefrontal cortex – bringing you *out* of reaction.

4. Find the Root

Ask:

"When was the first time I remember feeling this way?"

Let the memory come. That's your **origin wound.**

5. Reparent Yourself

Place a hand on your heart. Whisper:

"I see you. I love you. You're safe now."

You're not abandoning yourself anymore.

6. Choose Differently

Ask:

"What does my highest self want to do next?"

That's the power of transformation – **not reacting the way your past taught you to.**

Section 8.6: Communicating Your Triggers Without Losing People

Once you've regulated, **you can now connect.**

But most people either:

- Explode ("You're always disrespecting me!")
- Or collapse "It's fine... I'll just deal with it.")

The healthy way?

Own your experience without blame.

🧠 **The Script:**

"When that happened, I felt ___, and it reminded me of ___. I know it's my trigger, but I wanted to share so we can move forward with clarity."

This isn't weakness. It's **courageous vulnerability.**

It says:

- "I'm self-aware."
- "I want connection, not conflict."
- "I'm doing the inner work – and inviting you in."

📓 Section 8.7: Trigger Reflection Prompts

Use these journal prompts to decode your most common reactions:

1. *"What situations consistently trigger me?"*
2. *"What belief does that trigger reinforce?"*
3. *"Where did I first learn to feel this way?"*
4. *"How have I unconsciously passed this trigger onto others?"*
5. *"What would it feel like to respond instead of react?"*

"The moment you pause instead of explode – that's where healing lives."

📌 Chapter 8 Summary: You're Not Broken. You're Remembering.

Triggers don't mean you're failing.

They mean you're *ready to heal* what's been buried.

Your inner child doesn't need you to be perfect.

They need you to show up, speak gently, and create safety – from the inside out.

This chapter doesn't ask you to be emotionless.

It asks you to be **emotionally sovereign.**

That's not control.

That's **freedom.**

Chapter 9: The Shadow Self — Making Peace with the Parts You Hide

"You don't become enlightened by imagining figures of light, but by making the darkness conscious."

– Carl Jung

◆ 9.1 What Is the Shadow Self?

At its core, the **shadow self** is not evil, dangerous, or shameful – it is simply **unknown.**

Coined by Carl Jung, the "shadow" refers to the parts of ourselves we **repress, deny, or disown** because we were taught – explicitly or implicitly – that they were unacceptable.

But these disowned parts don't disappear. They go underground. They lurk beneath our thoughts, emotions, relationships, and behaviours, influencing us from the shadows.

"The shadow is everything about ourselves that we don't know yet. And it's trying to become known."

– Carl Jung

For example:

- A boy taught that "men don't cry" represses vulnerability. It becomes his shadow.
- A girl punished for being assertive hides her voice. It becomes her shadow.
- A teenager mocked for being weird hides their creativity. It becomes their shadow.

The shadow includes our:

- Unexpressed anger
- Disowned sexuality
- Envy we don't admit.
- Greed, we label "bad".
- Desires that feel taboo
- Wild, raw, unapologetic truths

The irony? Many of the things we bury... are also our greatest sources of power.

◆ 9.2 How the Shadow Is Formed

The shadow is born in childhood – through **social conditioning, cultural expectation**, and **emotional survival.**

A child is not born ashamed of who they are. They become ashamed because someone – a parent, teacher, peer, or society – taught them that part of them was **wrong, too much**, or **not enough**.

Some subtle (and not-so-subtle) shadow-creating messages:

- "You're too sensitive."
- "Don't get angry."
- "That's not ladylike."
- "Stop showing off."
- "Nice people don't say no."
- "You should always think of others first."

The child doesn't argue. They adapt.

They learn:

"In order to be loved, I have to **hide who I really am.**"

So, the self gets split:

- One part becomes the "persona" (the acceptable mask).
- The other part becomes the "shadow" (the banished truth).

This fragmentation leads to a life of:

- People-pleasing
- Perfectionism
- Emotional suppression
- Internal conflict
- Lack of fulfilment
- Relationship dysfunction

You can't love yourself if you're **cut off from half of yourself.**

◆ 9.3 Signs Your Shadow Is Running the Show

The shadow is not quiet. It finds ways to speak – through **reactions, compulsions, sabotage, and projections.**

Here are some red flags that your shadow is active:

🧠 1. Overreactions

You erupt in anger over a small comment. You cry unexpectedly in a meeting. You ghost someone after a compliment.

That's not the adult you. That's a shadow wound flaring up.

💬 2. Strong Judgements

You say things like:

- "She's such a narcissist."
- "He's too emotional."
- "They just want attention."
- Often, what we **judge harshly in others** reflects something we are **not at peace with in ourselves.**

🀄 3. Shame Spirals

You can't receive compliments. You obsess over tiny mistakes. You constantly replay what you said in social settings.

Your inner critic is the shadow's megaphone.

4. Sabotage Patterns

Just when things are going well – you ghost, procrastinate, pick a fight, and quit.

The shadow doesn't sabotage out of malice. It sabotages out of **fear** – fear that your success will expose what's still unhealed.

◆ 9.4 Shadow Projections – When You Judge What You Suppress

Projection is a defence mechanism where you **assign your shadow traits to others.**

Why?

Because it's easier to say, "They're arrogant" than to admit, "I'm afraid to own my confidence."

It's safer to say "They're fake" than to face your own discomfort with authenticity.

Example:

You judge your friend for being "too loud" and "attention-seeking".

Deep down, you're envious of their ability to speak freely – something **you never gave yourself permission to do.**

What triggers you in others... is often the part of *you* begging to be seen.

Shadow projection destroys relationships. It creates false enemies. It fuels gossip, resentment, and passive aggression.

The cure?

Radical self-honesty.

◆ 9.5 How to Do Shadow Work — A Gentle Descent

Shadow work is not:

- Endless self-criticism
- Obsessing over pain
- Becoming emotionally stoic

Shadow work is:

- **Curiosity over condemnation**
- **Compassion over judgement**
- **Wholeness over image**

🛠 Step-by-Step Shadow Work:

1. Identify the Pattern

What keeps happening in your life?

- Failed relationships?
- Burnout cycles?
- Trust issues?

Shadow says, "You haven't faced what's underneath."

2. Track the Emotional Charge

What makes you emotionally reactive?

- What comments make your blood boil?
- What traits in others disgust you?

Follow the heat. That's where the gold is buried.

3. Dialogue with the Shadow

Write a letter to the part of you you've exiled.

"Dear Shadow, I've ignored you. But I'm ready to hear you. What have you been trying to protect me from?"

Let it respond. Don't censor it. Let it rage, cry, scream, and laugh.

4. Reframe the Shadow Trait

Every "negative" trait holds wisdom:

- Anger = Boundary
- Jealousy = Desire
- Laziness = Overwhelm
- Control = Fear of chaos
- Arrogance = Repressed power

What gift is your shadow holding?

5. Reintegrate

Say to yourself:

"I allow myself to feel _______. I don't have to act on it. But I no longer shame it."

That's real freedom.

◆ 9.6 When the Shadow Is Integrated: You Become Whole

The goal of shadow work is not to become perfect.

It's to become **whole.**

When you make peace with your shadow:

- You stop needing external validation.
- You become less judgemental.
- You stop apologising for your truth.
- You move from reactivity to **sovereignty.**

You start to live as the full version of yourself:

- Bold
- Complex
- Honest
- Emotionally integrated
- Unshakeably grounded.

Your relationships improve.

Your creativity ignites.

Your purpose becomes clear.

You are no longer hiding in pieces. You are living in the present.

◆ 9.7 Shadow Self Reflection Prompts

These prompts are not for quick answers. They're for **depth.** Use them slowly. Revisit them often.

1. *What's a trait I secretly dislike in others – and why?*
2. *What emotion am I most uncomfortable expressing?*
3. *What am I afraid people will see if I stop performing?*
4. *What did I have to hide to be loved or accepted growing up?*
5. *What part of me still thinks I'm "too much" or "not enough"?*
6. *What do I want – but feel guilty for wanting?*
7. *Who would I be if I stopped hiding my full self?*

Chapter Summary: The Shadow Isn't the Enemy — It's the Ally

"Your shadow was never trying to destroy you. It was trying to protect you — with outdated instructions."

-- Anonymous

You are not a problem to be solved.

You are a **soul to be remembered.**

You are not too broken, too angry, too emotional, or too intense.

You are whole – and every shadow was just a **story waiting to be heard**.

When you stop hiding, you start **healing**.

And when you start healing, the world around you transforms.

Chapter 10: The Inner Voice — Rewriting the Script in Your Head

"The most important relationship you will ever have is the one you have with yourself – and the way you speak to yourself is how it lives."

~ Anonymous

◆ 10.1 The Voice You Hear the Most

Every morning, before the world says a word to you, a voice already has.

It's the one that says:

- "Get up; you're behind already."
- "You don't look good today."
- "Don't mess this up."
- "Why would they love someone like you?"

This voice doesn't shout. It whispers – constantly. It shapes your posture, your risk-taking, and your dreams.

Most of us never even notice it. We don't challenge it. We just assume:

"That's me."

But it's not.

That voice is **a recording** – built from thousands of interactions, expectations, rejections, shames, rules, and fears.

Your inner voice is either:

- A coach that fuels your courage

- Or a tyrant that depletes your spirit

You're not just living life.

You're living the **story your voice talks about. Life.**

And that means – you can **rewrite the narrative.**

◆ 10.2 Where Does the Inner Critic Come From?

The inner critic wasn't born with you.

It was **trained into you.**

A child doesn't second-guess their value. Watch any toddler:

- They'll sing off-key with joy.
- They'll dance even when no one's watching.
- They'll cry when they need help and laugh when they're proud.

But slowly, the world begins to say:

- "Tone it down."
- "Don't act out."
- "Stop crying."
- "Be realistic."
- "That's not how a man/woman should behave."

The child doesn't argue. The child **adapts.**

They internalise the rules. And the rules become a **voice.**

That voice becomes the filter:

- "Don't speak up; they'll laugh."
- "Don't try that; you'll fail."
- "Don't be emotional; that's weakness."

What we call *self-talk* is often just *old survival conditioning.*

But you're not a child anymore.

You don't need that kind of protection.

It's time to reclaim the mic.

◆ 10.3 The Three Types of Inner Voices

The Inner Critic (Shame-Driven)

Most common. Most destructive.

Main Script:

"You're too much. You're not enough. You're a failure waiting to happen."

It's not motivating. It's paralysing.

It confuses cruelty with accountability.

It kills joy. It feeds perfectionism. It fears rejection.

The Inner Protector (Fear-Driven)

This voice sounds like safety. But it's built on fear.

Main Script:

"Don't take risks. Don't get vulnerable. Don't trust too much."

It's the voice that plays it small.

It's the one that walks away first, so it doesn't get abandoned.

It hides behind logic – but it's terrified of exposure.

The Inner Wall (Numbness-Driven)

This voice doesn't attack or caution – it **disconnects.**

Main Script:

"Whatever. Who cares? Just survive."

It grew out of burnout. Grief. Repeated disappointment.

It builds walls so thick... Even your dreams can't find a way in.

But all three of these voices? **They're not evil. They're scared. And outdated.**

◆ 10.4 Neuroplasticity – You Can Rewire the Voice

Let's talk science – because this isn't just motivational fluff.

You can literally rewire your mind.

Through **neuroplasticity**, your brain can:

- Grow new connections!
- Reorganise thought patterns!
- Dismantle unhelpful beliefs.
- Create new default responses.

Every thought you think **creates or strengthens a neural pathway.**

So, if your daily thoughts are:

"I'm a screw-up" or "I'll never succeed" – you are **rehearsing your limitations.**

But if you start thinking:

"I'm not there yet, but I'm growing" or "My story isn't over" – you're **rehearsing resilience.**

🧠 **Try this:**

When a critical voice speaks, pause and ask:

- "Who taught me this tone?"
- "Is this voice helping or harming?"
- "What voice does my healed self want to hear right now?"

Then **say it. Aloud. On purpose.**

Because **what you say becomes what you believe** – and eventually, how you live.

◆ 10.5 Rewriting Prompts for the Inner Voice

These prompts are the scaffolding to **rebuild your inner language.**

Don't just read them – use them. Live them.

OLD: "I'm too behind in life."

NEW: "I'm on my own path, not theirs. And I move at my own divine pace."

OLD: "They'll think I'm stupid."

NEW: "My courage to speak isn't about their comfort. It's about my truth."

OLD: "What if I fail?"

NEW: "What if I fly? What if this changes everything?"

OLD: "I always mess up relationships."

NEW: "I'm learning. Healing. And love is a journey, not a performance."

You are allowed to be **both healing and worthy.**

Don't wait to be perfect before you speak kindly to yourself.

◆ 10.6 Talking Back to Shame – And Winning

Shame thrives in silence.

It whispers:

- "You're not loveable."
- "If they really knew you..."
- "You're a burden. A fraud."

Shame wants isolation. Because connection **dismantles** it.

So how do we break shame's grip?

With **compassionate truth-telling.**

Anti-Shame Statements:

- "My mistakes are not my identity."
- "I am allowed to be both messy and magical."
- "Healing doesn't mean pretending it never hurt."
- "I'm allowed to begin again – as many times as I need."

Talk back to shame with the **voice your younger self needed to hear.**

◆ 10.7 The Inner Voice in Relationships

Your self-talk isn't just yours.

It bleeds into how you **see others**, **communicate**, and **receive love.**

Examples:

- If you believe "I'm a burden" → You'll apologise for having needs.
- If you believe "I'll be abandoned" → You'll push people away first.
- If you believe "I'm unloveable" → You'll settle for crumbs and call it a feast.

Your relationships don't start with others.

They start with your inner script.

So, to change your patterns, you must change your **inner narrator.**

◆ 10.8 Pause & Reflect: Reclaim the Mic

Grab a journal. Speak truth.

1. What's the harshest thing I say to myself regularly?
2. Who did I first hear that from in my life?
3. What did I need to hear instead?
4. How can I begin saying that to myself now – daily?

5. What voice does my future self speak with? Can I borrow that now?

"Your voice shapes yourself. Be intentional. Be compassionate. Be brave."

📌 Chapter 10 Summary: The Voice Becomes the World

"Change doesn't begin with the world. It begins with the words we say to ourselves in the dark."

Your mind is a home.

Your inner voice is the interior designer.

If you want peace, paint the walls in compassion.

If you want joy – open the windows to possibility.

If you want safety – lock the doors to shame.

And if you want to **feel whole again** –

Speak like someone worth loving.

Because you are.

And the world hears you loudest... when you **finally hear yourself.**

Chapter 11: Self-Sabotage — Why You Block Your Own Light and How to Stop

"Your comfort zone is a beautifully decorated prison where your dreams go to die."

- Anonymous

◆ 11.1 What Is Self-Sabotage?

Self-sabotage is not laziness.

It's not weakness.

It's not a personality flaw.

It's **a survival strategy** – coded into your nervous system when **success, love, or visibility felt dangerous.**

You procrastinate not because you're unmotivated...

But because finishing the task might expose you to judgement, failure, or even praise you're not ready to receive.

You ghost people not because you don't care...

But because intimacy activates old wounds of abandonment.

You overthink every move not because you're "a perfectionist"...

But because somewhere in your past, making a mistake cost you *love.*

Self-sabotage is the inner child pulling the fire alarm because the adult self is about to walk into a room it doesn't feel safe in.

◆ 11.2 The Psychology of Self-Sabotage

At the heart of self-sabotage is this chilling paradox:

"I want change... but I'm afraid of what change will demand of me."

🔍 **Key Psychological Roots:**

🧠 1. Fear of Success

Sounds counterintuitive, right? But here's the truth: success requires visibility. Responsibility. Risk. For someone raised to equate attention with punishment or shame, success can feel like danger.

😔 2. Low Self-Worth

You subconsciously don't believe you deserve happiness, ease, or love – so when you get close, you ruin it.

😨 3. Attachment Wounds

If relationships used to mean chaos or abandonment, your nervous system might destroy connection before it has a chance to betray you.

🔄 4. Familiar Pain Is Safer Than Unknown Peace

The brain craves *familiarity*, not happiness. If you were raised in criticism, silence, or chaos, you will **recreate those dynamics**, even in peaceful spaces, because they feel normal.

◆ 11.3 How Self-Sabotage Shows Up in Real Life

You might not call it self-sabotage...

But it hides in plain sight.

🔥 **Common Forms:**

- Chronic procrastination on meaningful goals
- Staying in toxic relationships
- Ghosting clients or partners before big moments
- Starting projects and never finishing
- Downplaying your talent
- Choosing comfort over growth
- Emotional eating, overspending, bingeing

🔍 **Patterns to Look For:**

- *"Every time I'm close to a breakthrough, something goes wrong."*
- *"I always date the same type of person – and it never works out."*
- *"I talk myself out of everything good."*

These aren't failures.

They're patterns.

And patterns are **stories with roots.**

◆ 11.4 The Biology of Sabotage – Your Nervous System and the Safety Trap

Your nervous system's job is not to make you successful.

It's to **keep you safe.**

If it associates visibility, intimacy, or achievement with pain – it will trigger defence mechanisms:

Fight-Flight-Freeze-Fawn:

- **Fight:** You pick fights, get defensive, and push away success.
- **Flight:** You quit, ghost, procrastinate
- **Freeze:** You go numb, overthink, and binge-watch.
- **Fawn:** You overgive, people-please, and lose your voice.

The nervous system doesn't care if you're thriving.

It only cares if you're **surviving in familiar conditions.**

"Healing is teaching your nervous system that joy isn't dangerous."

◆ 11.5 Shadow Sabotage – When Unconscious Parts Hijack the Mission

Remember the Shadow Self from Chapter 9?

Self-sabotage is often **your shadow pulling strings behind the curtain.**

The parts you haven't integrated – your jealousy, shame, rage, and power – they leak out by:

- Making you shrink in important moments.
- Whispering lies like "you'll fail anyway".
- Driving impulsive, destructive choices

"If you don't make peace with your shadow... it will burn your life down just to be seen."

◆ 11.6 The Upper Limit Problem – Why You Fear Too Much Good

Gay Hendricks calls it the **Upper Limit Problem:**

The point at which joy, love, or success becomes so unfamiliar... your self-sabotage to return to a tolerable emotional temperature.

Examples:

- You get a promotion → Pick a fight with your partner.
- You hit a fitness goal → Binge the next day.
- You feel deeply loved → Suddenly pull away.

You're not ruining good things because you're broken.

You're doing it because **your thermostat was set for suffering.**

It's time to **raise your capacity to receive good things** – without guilt, anxiety, or sabotage.

◆ 11.7 How to Stop Sabotaging Your Own Greatness

🧘 Step 1: Build Awareness Without Shame

Don't beat yourself up. Observe.

Ask:

- "What was I feeling right before I sabotaged?"
- "What part of me felt threatened?"

- "What outcome am I subconsciously avoiding?"

✍ Step 2: Track Your Triggers

Keep a "sabotage journal".

Every time you catch a pattern, log:

- The situation
- Your reaction
- The emotion underneath
- The belief driving it.

🧠 Step 3: Speak to the Inner Saboteur

This part of you is not evil – it's scared. Write:

"Dear saboteur, what are you afraid will happen if I succeed?"

Listen. Then reply with compassion:

"Thank you for protecting me. But we don't live in that danger anymore."

🔁 Step 4: Rewire Through Repetition

Practice:

- Celebrating success *without* disclaimers
- Sitting with joy without checking for the exit
- Staying in intimacy without pulling away
- Committing to habits *even when uncomfortable*

Healing happens in the **micro-moments you choose courage over comfort.**

◆ 11.8 Journal Prompts to Disarm Self-Sabotage

1. *What do I believe will happen if I fully succeed?*
2. *What am I afraid of losing if I grow?*

3. *Where did I learn that joy/success/love wasn't safe?*
4. *How have I sabotaged myself in the past, and what was I trying to protect myself from?*
5. *What does my life look like if I stop getting in my own way?*
6. *What version of me is still stuck in survival – and what does it need to feel safe now?*

📌 Chapter 11 Summary – You Are Not Broken. You Are Buried Beneath Defence.

You're not lazy.

You're not a quitter.

You're not inconsistent.

You're not impossible.

You are someone who learnt – at some point – that good things hurt.

And now, it's time to teach yourself that **you can be safe in success.**

You can be seen without shame.

You can be loved without loss.

You can grow without guilt.

You can rise without running.

"Stop lighting your life on fire just to stay warm in the familiar."

It's your time. Turn off the alarm.

Chapter 12: Reparenting the Inner Child — The Healing Your Past Was Waiting For

"You can't change your childhood. But you can change how it lives inside of you." ~ Anonymous

◆ 12.1 What Is the Inner Child?

The inner child is the **living archive of your earliest emotional experiences** — it's the echo of every praise and punishment, every bedtime story and betrayal, every "you're enough" and every silent night without comfort.

Anecdote:

Riya, a 35-year-old therapist, used to freeze whenever someone raised their voice. It didn't matter if the words weren't meant to hurt — her body remembered her father yelling during her childhood. That's the inner child: **a sensory memory of emotional truth.**

Even decades later, your inner child can dictate:

- The way you love.
- The way you fear abandonment.
- The way you speak (or don't speak) your truth.

It's not about age regression.

It's about **acknowledging the child inside you who never felt safe — and letting them know that now, you are their safety.**

◆ 12.2 Why Reparenting Is the Most Powerful Inner Work

Reparenting is the conscious act of **becoming the parent your younger self needed.**

We often inherit parenting styles that reflect emotional scarcity – not because our parents were evil, but because **they too were unparented children** in grown-up bodies.

"Until you make peace with your past, your inner child will run your future."

Reparenting empowers you to:

- Offer **validation instead of shame.**
- Set **boundaries instead of barriers.**
- Speak **compassion instead of criticism.**

Case Study:

Arjun, a senior leader in a global firm, couldn't tolerate feedback. In therapy, he discovered this reaction came from being constantly compared to his older brother. Reparenting taught him to receive feedback without associating it with unworthiness. The result? He became a more grounded leader – and a father who praises effort, not just results.

◆ 12.3 The Four Core Needs of the Inner Child

1. Safety

"I need to feel protected – not punished."

Lack of safety as a child often results in hypervigilance or emotional numbness as an adult.

Anecdote:

Jasmin, now 27, shared how unpredictable her alcoholic mother was. Every door slam still makes her flinch. Through reparenting, she learned grounding techniques, like pressing her palms together while repeating: "That was then. This is now. I am safe."

2. Attunement

"I need someone to notice how I feel – not dismiss it."

Attunement is about **emotional presence**, not just physical care.

Case Study:

Leo, raised in a "boys don't cry" household, became a stoic adult. His relationships suffered – he couldn't express joy or grief. Reparenting for him meant allowing tears during solo journaling. Today, he says, "I'm not soft. I'm whole."

3. Boundaries

"I need structure and protection – not control."

Children who were over-parented or under-parented struggle with boundaries:

- Over-parented = Rebel or collapse
- Under-parented = Overextend to feel worthy

Anecdote:

Megha, a school principal, always said yes – even when exhausted. Her reparenting journey included practicing "No" in the mirror until it felt natural. "Saying no doesn't make me cruel – it makes me whole," she says.

4. Encouragement

"I need to be celebrated – not compared."

Children who only received love for accomplishments grow into **adults who fear rest.**

Case Study:

Rajiv, a startup founder, faced burnout. His therapist traced it back to being called "lazy" when he rested as a child. Reparenting meant scheduling joy without guilt. "I now rest like it's sacred," he says.

◆ 12.4 How to Begin the Reparenting Process

This is not a one-day fix.

This is **emotional archaeology** – and resurrection.

Step 1: Meet Your Inner Child

Sit quietly. Picture them.

- What's their name?
- How do they sit?
- What do their eyes say?

Then say:

"Hi. I'm here now. And I'm not going anywhere."

Step 2: Write to Them

Journal Prompt:

"Dear younger me, I know you were never heard. But I hear you now. What are you still holding?"

Let the answer come from within. Don't judge it. Just honour it.

Step 3: Give What Was Missing

Were you never hugged? Hug yourself – tight, real, long.

Was your voice silenced? Start recording affirmations in your own voice.

Give them now what they were denied then.

Step 4: Rewire the Narrative

Write:

"I was taught that love looks like _______. But I now know love is _______."

Do this often. Beliefs need **repetition to become reality.**

◆ 12.5 When Inner Child Wounds Go Unhealed

Unhealed children show up in boardrooms, bedrooms, and breakdowns.

Adult Symptoms:

- Overachieving to prove worth
- Avoiding intimacy due to fear of betrayal
- Distrusting joy
- Mistaking anxiety for intuition
- Self-sacrificing to avoid abandonment.

"If you don't speak to your inner child, your adult life will become their scream."

◆ 12.6 Case Reflections: Real Stories of Inner Healing

Case 1: The Smiling Overachiever

Nikita, 30, couldn't stop working. Success was her drug – and she still felt empty.

In therapy, she discovered her father only praised her when she achieved something. She had become a "performance machine." Through reparenting, she learned to **sit in stillness without shame**. Now, her biggest flex is: "I don't hustle to be loved."

Case 2: The Quiet People-Pleaser

Ali, 40, would do anything to avoid conflict. Raised in a home with explosive fights, he learned to appease everyone. Reparenting taught him that **boundaries are not betrayal** – they are **bridges to self-respect**.

Today, Ali's mantra: "I disappoint others, so I don't keep disappointing myself."

🧩 Case 3: The Fierce Controller

Sneha, a high-performing lawyer, micro-managed everything. Underneath? A childhood where chaos reigned – divorce, relocations, neglect.

Reparenting let her loosen her grip: "Control was my armour. I don't need it anymore to feel safe."

◆ 12.7 The Neuroscience of Reparenting

You're not just healing emotionally.

You're **rewiring your brain**.

- Each loving thought forms **new neural links**
- Each self-kindness increases **vagal tone** (rest/digest system)
- Each safe emotional experience increases **resilience under stress.**

You're not pretending. You're programming.

Not escaping the past – but **integrating it with grace.**

◆ 12.8 Journal Prompts for Inner Child Reconnection

These are **soul excavators**:

1. *What did I most want to hear as a child?*
2. *How did I feel when I expressed emotions as a child?*
3. *What am I afraid will happen if I stop over-functioning?*
4. *Which adult patterns do I now see were born from childhood defence?*
5. *What does my inner child want me to know right now?*

Let them answer. Don't censor. Don't rush. **Feel it. Then heal it.**

📌 Chapter 12 Summary – The Parent Within

"You don't need a time machine to heal the past. You just need a mirror and a moment of courage." ~ Anonymous

You are not too broken.

You are not too late.

You are not "too sensitive."

You are someone who has carried pain for too long – in silence.

And now, that silence breaks.

You become the home.

You become the embrace.

You become the voice that whispers:

"You were always worthy.

Even when no one told you."

Chapter 13: The Art of Emotional Safety — Creating Space for Truth in Relationships

"In the absence of emotional safety, truth whispers. In its presence, truth sings." – Anonymous

◆ 13.1 What Is Emotional Safety?

Emotional safety is the **invisible permission slip** we offer others to be authentic – without fear of punishment, ridicule, or abandonment. It is not comfort. It is not pacification. It is **freedom with protection.**

In emotionally safe environments, we say:

- "I don't have to censor myself."
- "I can be wrong and still be loved."
- "My presence is welcome – not a performance."

Emotional safety is **co-created**, not assumed. And in its absence:

- Connection becomes compliance.
- Vulnerability feels like danger.
- Intimacy becomes a battlefield of self-doubt.

Anecdote:

Dr. Sameer, a trauma therapist, recalls a couple he once worked with:

"Every time the wife shared something emotional, the husband made a joke. It wasn't cruelty – it was fear. His father mocked him for crying. Humour became armour. We had to build safety before we could build understanding."

◆ 13.2 Why Emotional Safety Is the Oxygen of Every Relationship

You can't build intimacy, creativity, or healing without safety.

Without it:

- Clients lie to their therapists.
- Students shut down in classrooms.
- Partners withhold their truths.
- Children walk on eggshells at home.

With it:

- People take risks.
- Vulnerability feels sacred.
- Growth becomes possible.

Case Study:

Dr. Leena Desai, a school psychologist, implemented emotional safety protocols in a school with high suspension rates. Teachers were trained in trauma-informed responses, active listening, and emotional regulation.

In a year:

- Suspensions dropped by 43%.
- Student trust ratings in staff increased by 70%.
- One child said: "This is the first place I don't get in trouble just for being upset."

That's the power of psychological safety in action.

◆ 13.3 The Five Pillars of Emotional Safety (*Blended with Case Layers*)

🧭 1. Non-Reactivity

People don't open if you explode, mock, or withdraw.

"Be a mirror, not a megaphone."

Example:

Ravi, a marriage counsellor, noticed that one partner would flinch when interrupted. Why? Her father screamed every time she disagreed. Ravi coached the husband to pause and reflect instead of reacting. Within 6 weeks, she said, "I finally exhaled in this relationship."

🔐 2. Confidentiality

What is shared in trust, stays sacred.

"If they have to fear your mouth, they'll never trust your heart."

Example:

A senior HR leader shared her trauma in a coaching circle. Days later, a peer referenced it casually. She never spoke again in group meetings. Emotional safety broken once can take **years to rebuild**.

🤲 3. Validation Over Solution

You don't fix. You feel with.

"The emotionally safe response is not 'here's what you should do' – it's 'I get why that hurts.'"

Therapist Insight:

Dr. Mitali Bhat, a licensed psychotherapist, says:

"Clients don't want logic first. They want their inner world mirrored back. Once they feel seen, then they can hear options."

🧱 4. Boundaried Compassion

You can say "no" and still be deeply kind.

"Compassion without boundaries becomes martyrdom. Boundaries without compassion become walls."

Relationship Reflection:

Karim, a relationship coach, teaches couples:

"You don't need to say yes to everything to be emotionally available. Being clear is being kind."

🔄 5. Emotional Consistency

Erratic behaviour is terrifying. Predictability is peace.

"Don't make people guess which version of you they're getting today."

Case Study:

A teenage girl in group therapy said:

"My dad was either my hero or a hurricane. I learned to never show emotion – because it could trigger either."

Now, as an adult, she distrusts peace.

Because it once preceded a storm.

◆ 13.4 How to Create Emotional Safety in Practice (*With Clinical Tools & Stories*)

🧘 1. Pause Before Responding

Ask:

"Am I about to protect them, or protect my ego?"

Application in Therapy:

Therapists often use a grounding breath before responding to heavy disclosures. This brief pause honours **regulation over reaction.**

🛠 2. Repair After Rupture

No one gets it perfect. What builds safety is **repair.**

Say:

- "That didn't come out right. Let me try again."
- "I hear your pain – not just your words."

Emotional safety is not built on perfection – it's built on **integrity after the mess.**

🎤 3. Invite, Don't Instruct

Instead of saying "You need to..."

Say: "Would it feel okay if we explored...?"

Emotional safety invites the person to step forward – not corner them into a confession.

◆ 13.5 Emotional Safety in Relationships: Romantic, Familial, and Therapeutic

❤ Romantic:

- Validate emotions before solutions.
- Don't use vulnerabilities against each other.
- Be consistent in tone and affection.

"Safety is the sexiest thing in a relationship. It makes intimacy possible."

🏠 Familial:

- Model apology
- Show emotion without shame.
- Avoid gaslighting phrases: "You're too sensitive," "That never happened".

"What kids call love is often just the emotional availability they were allowed to see."

🧑⚕️ **Therapeutic:**

- Always ask for consent before deep work
- Let clients know it's okay to push back.
- Mirror, don't manufacture.

"Therapists who model humility build deeper safety than therapists who try to look all-knowing."

◆ 13.6 Emotional Safety in Professional and Educational Settings

🧑🏫 **In Education:**

Safe classrooms teach:

- Mistakes are learning.
- All emotions are welcome.
- No child is punished for expression.

Teacher Testimony:

Ms. Devika, a trauma-sensitive educator, says:

"When I stopped reacting to disrespect and started asking 'What happened today?' – my students started telling the truth."

👩 **In Leadership:**

Safe teams innovate more because:

- They aren't punished for failure.
- They don't hide errors.
- They feel respected for authenticity.

"Leaders who say, 'I don't know – what do you think?' are the ones who build genius rooms."

◆ 13.7 Journal Prompts for Self-Reflection on Safety

1. *What part of me still feels unsafe to be seen fully?*
2. *When did someone make me feel deeply safe – what did they do?*
3. *When have I broken someone's emotional safety – how can I repair it?*
4. *Where do I feel I'm walking on eggshells in my life?*
5. *What version of me is hiding because it wasn't once safe to show up?*

📌 Chapter 13 Summary – Safety Is Sacred

"People heal where they feel safe. They thrive where they feel seen. They stay where they feel valued." ~ Anonymous

Safety isn't fluffy. It's **foundational.**

It creates:

- Leaders who listen.
- Partners who nurture.
- Therapists who transform.
- Families who unlearn fear
- Communities who hold each other

In a world addicted to noise, be the person who listens.

In a world obsessed with performance, be the place where people can **finally be real.**

Chapter 14: Emotional Boundaries — The Art of Protecting Your Peace Without Losing Your People

"Boundaries aren't rejection. They are direction. They show others how to reach the real you – respectfully."

-- Anonymous

◆ 14.1 What Are Emotional Boundaries?

Emotional boundaries are the invisible, yet powerful guidelines we create to define:

- What we're responsible for emotionally
- How others may treat us
- Where our energy begins and ends

They are how we say:

"I am willing to connect, but I will not be consumed."

Without boundaries, people:

- Overextend themselves.
- Absorb emotions that aren't theirs
- Lose clarity in relationships.

With boundaries, they reclaim:

- Emotional sovereignty
- Relational clarity
- Inner peace

Anecdote:

Ananya, a trauma recovery coach, realized she was emotionally absorbing the pain of every client. She felt physically sick after sessions. When she learned to say, "This is yours, and I honour it – but I don't carry it," she transformed. Not only did her health improve, but her clients became more empowered too – because **she modelled energetic clarity.**

◆ 14.2 Why Boundaries Are Sacred for Mental and Relational Health

Unboundaried compassion becomes co-dependency.

Unboundaried availability becomes burnout.

Boundaries are not cold. They're **honest.**

They allow for **sustainable connection** – not performative sacrifice.

Clinical Case Study:

Dr. Karthik, a clinical psychologist, found himself resenting his clients. After deep supervision work, he realized he hadn't enforced time boundaries – sessions ran long, texts came at midnight.

He restructured:

- No-contact hours.
- Session caps
- A therapeutic container with rituals to "close the session".

His emotional fatigue disappeared. His clients flourished. He said:

"When I respected my limits, I finally taught them to respect theirs."

◆ 14.3 The Different Types of Emotional Boundaries (with Deeper Application)

◆ 1. Verbal Boundaries

You teach people how to **speak to you** – not just what to say.

Example: "If the conversation becomes sarcastic or disrespectful, I'll Walk away."

🌟Reflection:

Think of how tone was used in your childhood home. If yelling was normalized, you may not know you have a right to ask for calm. You do.

◆ 2. Energetic Boundaries

How much of someone else's emotion do you absorb? Feel responsible for?

Example: "I hold space – but I don't soak in your pain."

🎤Anecdote:

Yusuf, an energy healer, visualizes a "zip-up suit of light" before every session. It keeps him energetically present, not entangled.

◆ 3. Identity Boundaries

You are allowed to be **you**, even when others disagree.

Example: "My identity and values aren't up for debate."

🔬 Therapist Tip:

Boundaries here are crucial for clients from marginalized communities navigating family systems that shame their truth (e.g., LGBTQ+, spiritual awakening, neurodivergent traits).

◆ 4. Time and Availability Boundaries

How you manage your energy is how you manage your life.

Example: "I need Sundays for rest. Let's connect Monday."

🛑 Burnout Red Flag:

If your calendar looks full – but your spirit feels empty – you don't have time management issues. You have **boundary wounds.**

◆ 14.4 How Boundary Violations Damage Relationships

Common Forms:

- Guilt-tripping someone for needing space.
- Over-texting without consent
- Mocking someone's emotional expression.
- Asking invasive questions and calling it "honesty"
- Expecting emotional labour from friends/partners without reciprocity

🧠 Deep Dive:

Violation often comes from **fear, not malice.**

But fear is no excuse for boundary-bulldozing.

📌 Clinical Case:

Lena, a psychotherapist, worked with a client whose husband would check her texts, criticize her outfits, and call it "concern."

Through boundary work, Lena's client learned to say:

"Your insecurity is valid. Your control is not."

That sentence saved her autonomy – and her marriage found healing when he did his own work.

◆ 14.5 How to Set Boundaries Without Guilt, Fear, or Rage

Setting a boundary is an **act of clarity, not cruelty.**

Step-by-Step Strategy:

1. **Name the discomfort:** "I feel drained after long calls."
2. **Identify the boundary:** "I need to limit phone time to 20 minutes."
3. **State it clearly:** "Let's chat 20 minutes and pause till tomorrow."

4. **Enforce it kindly:** "Hey, I'm ending the call now – I'll message you tomorrow."

🔄 **Reframe Guilt:**

"This isn't mean. This is me being honest about what I can sustain."

✨ **Anecdote:**

Rohit, a young dad and tech lead, felt guilty telling his boss no. Until his wife said,

"Every yes to them is a no to us."

That was his wake-up call.

◆ 14.6 Boundary Setting in Different Roles .

Boundaries are not one-size-fits-all.

They are **contextual**, shaped by the role, the relationship, and the emotional history attached.

Let's explore what healthy boundary-setting looks like in **specific life roles**, with tailored language, tools, and common traps.

🩺 A. For Healthcare Workers and Mental Health Professionals

Why it matters:

Caregivers often operate in emotional intensity zones. Without boundaries, empathy becomes emotional bleeding. Burnout follows.

Common Pitfalls:

- Taking emotional calls off-hours
- Not separating identity from patient outcomes
- Over functioning out of guilt

Boundary Strategies:

- Use scripts:

"Let's continue this in our next appointment."

"For urgent needs, please use the emergency contact protocol."

- Create a **visual decompression routine**:

Between sessions, light a candle, stretch, or journal for 3 minutes to clear energetic residue.

💼 B. For Leaders, Managers, and Founders

Why it matters:

Leadership without emotional boundaries leads to blurred lines, favouritism, burnout, or toxic productivity.

Common Pitfalls:

- Texting team at night/weekends
- Rewarding overwork
- Over-functioning for underperformers

Boundary Strategies:

- Culture codes: "We don't chase people after hours unless it's urgent."
- Lead by example: "I take lunch breaks and vacations – I expect you to do the same."
- Clarity in roles and delegation

Manager's Mantra:

"I'm not a firefighter. I'm a builder of boundaries that allow fire to be controlled."

🎓 C. For Teachers, Coaches, and Educators

Why it matters:

Students learn boundaries by watching them modelled. Educators who collapse boundaries teach students to blur their own.

Common Pitfalls:

- Being emotionally available 24/7
- Allowing parent intrusions into personal life
- Over giving beyond the job scope

Boundary Strategies:

- Clarify support windows: "Office hours are Monday to Friday, 10–5."
- Use "empathy scripts" that keep boundaries intact:

"That sounds tough. I can listen now for 10 minutes, then we'll find a plan."

Educator's Ethic:

"Holding space doesn't mean holding the weight."

💞 D. For Romantic Relationships

Why it matters:

Without boundaries, love becomes enmeshment. Intimacy requires **separation with connection** – not merging.

Common Pitfalls:

- Mistaking control for closeness
- Weaponizing silence when boundaries are set.
- Confusing emotional labour with love

Boundary Strategies:

- Shared rituals: "No phones during dinner."
- Emotional check-ins: "Is there something I've done that crossed a line for you lately?"

Partner's Promise:

"I choose you. But I will not lose myself to love you."

👪 E. For Parents (of Young and Grown Children)

Why it matters:

Parents must model self-respect. Children imitate boundary health – not boundary talk.

Common Pitfalls:

- Overparenting grown children.
- Invading emotional privacy
- Forcing emotional dependence in the name of love

Boundary Strategies:

- Respect emotional privacy: "Would you like comfort, advice, or space?"
- Set tech boundaries: "I won't respond to messages after 9PM unless it's urgent."

Parent's Affirmation:

"My child is not mine to control – they are mine to respect, guide, and release."

◆ 14.7 Common Boundary Fears – and How to Rewire Them .

Every boundary you struggle to set is attached to an old **emotional story**.

Let's dismantle the most common fears – and install **healthy rewrites** rooted in safety and truth.

🔥 Fear #1: "If I set a boundary, they'll leave me."

Root:

Usually born from early abandonment wounds – a parent who left, or love that was withdrawn when you had needs.

Rewire:

"If someone walks away because I express a need, they were holding love hostage — not offering it freely."

Script:

"If this connection requires my silence to survive, it's not a connection. It's captivity."

Fear #2: "I'll be seen as selfish or cold."

Root:

Comes from environments where self-sacrifice was glorified. Where burnout was mistaken for love.

Rewire:

"It is not selfish to choose self-respect. It's sacred."

Script:

"My boundary is not rejection. It's redirection — toward sustainable connection."

Fear #3: "They'll think I'm difficult or dramatic."

Root:

Born from gaslighting — often in environments where expressing needs or emotion got you labelled "too much."

Rewire:

"If honouring my truth makes others uncomfortable, that discomfort is not mine to carry."

Script:

"The right people won't punish me for needing space. They'll protect it with me."

🔥 Fear #4: "But they need me."

Root:

Co-dependency and childhood enmeshment. You were rewarded for being the emotional caretaker.

Rewire:

"Support doesn't mean saviour. I am not responsible for carrying what others won't own."

Script:

"I'm here to help – not to be hollowed out."

🔥 Fear #5: "They won't understand."

Root:

Often learned in families where emotion was shut down. Speaking up never led to clarity – only punishment.

Rewire:

"Understanding isn't guaranteed. Respect can exist even without agreement."

Script:

"My clarity matters more than their comfort."

🎯 Final Note:

You don't owe anyone:

- Constant access
- An explanation for your peace
- A version of you that erases yourself to keep them comfortable.

"The people who get upset when you set boundaries are often the ones who benefited most when you had none."

📌 Chapter 14 Summary – Boundaries Aren't Walls. They're Windows.

"Boundaries don't break connection. They build authentic ones."

~ Anonymous

You don't need to:

- Say yes to be loved.
- Suffer to be worthy.
- Shrink to fit a relationship.

Boundaries say:

"Here is where I end and begin.

And you are welcome – if you respect the line."

Chapter 15: Resilience Rewired — How to Bounce Back Without Breaking Down

"Resilience isn't about staying strong. It's about staying whole – even when you've been broken."

~ Anonymous

◆ 15.1 What Is Resilience — Really?

Resilience is not "toughness."

It's not "positive vibes only."

It's the **capacity to face adversity, metabolize it emotionally, and still choose forward motion.**

It's the psychological equivalent of saying:

"This didn't break me – it taught me where I was already whole."

Resilience is the **mindset, the mechanism, and the map** we use to turn pain into power.

🔑Anecdote:

Allen, 27, survived a toxic workplace and severe burnout. In therapy, she said:

"I kept pushing through, calling it resilience. But I was just numbing out and collapsing silently."

That's not resilience. That's survival.

True resilience means feeling the pain, facing the fear, and **choosing conscious recovery.**

◆ 15.2 The Neuroscience of Resilience

Resilience is deeply wired into our **neurobiology:**

- The **prefrontal cortex** helps us reason through distress.
- The **amygdala** triggers our fear or fight-flight response.
- The **hippocampus** helps regulate memory and perspective during trauma.

💡 **Neuroplasticity:**

Your brain can literally **restructure itself** based on how you interpret and respond to stress.

"Every challenge faced with curiosity builds new wiring. Every emotional regulation moment is a brain workout."

◆ 15.3 Traits of Highly Resilient People

Not born. **Built.**

Resilient individuals cultivate:

1. 🧠 **Cognitive Flexibility** – "Maybe this isn't the end – just a pivot point."
2. 💬 **Emotional Agility** – "These hurts, but I'll move with it – not against it."
3. 🙏 **Support Seeking** – "I'm not weak for needing help. I'm wise."
4. **Self-Compassion** – "Even if I failed, I still deserve grace."
5. 🔍 **Meaning-Making** – "This pain will not be wasted. I'll extract wisdom."

CASE STUDY 1: Arun – The Executive Who Lost His Job and Found His Calling

Context: Arun, a 48-year-old senior executive at a multinational firm, was let go after a surprise merger. He had built his identity on title, salary, and status. Overnight, it all crumbled.

Initial Spiral:

- Shame spiralled into isolation.
- He couldn't face his family.
- His confidence collapsed.

Therapeutic Turning Point:

His therapist said:

"Arun, what if this wasn't a rejection – but a redirection?"

That phrase cracked him open. He began journaling, running, meditating. He took online coaching certifications, something he'd shelved for years.

Outcome:

Six months later, Arun launched a leadership coaching company.

His first client? The very company that let him go.

He said:

"I walked in not with revenge – but with renewal. I wasn't the man they let go. I was the man I became because they did."

◆ 15.4 The Five Phases of Real Resilience

1. Shock – "What just happened?"

Your body freezes. Your brain screams. This is trauma's doorway.

2. Disorientation – "Who am I without this?"

Grief, confusion, identity collapse. Normal.

3. Meaning-Making – "What is life asking me to learn here?"

Journaling. Reflection. Asking deeper questions.

4. Skill-Building – "What tools do I need now?"

Therapy. Coaching. Coping. Habits. Boundaries.

5. Re-Integration – "This shaped me — but it does not define me."

You don't bounce back. You bounce **forward, up,** and **through.**

◆ 15.5 Resilience vs. Suppression

Suppression: "I'm fine." (But you're numb.)

Resilience: "I'm not okay — but I'm growing anyway."

CASE STUDY 2: Janice — The Doctor Who Shattered Over a Coffee Spill

Context: Janice was a paediatrician. Respected. Relentless. Unshakeable.

Until one morning, she spilled her coffee and broke down sobbing.

What Triggered It:

It wasn't the coffee. It was 16 years of:

- Bottled grief from losing patients.
- Endless 20-hour shifts
- No space to cry, to crack, to be.

What Saved Her:

Her supervisor walked in, held her hand and whispered,

"It's okay to fall apart. You've held too much for too long."

That day, Janice took a sabbatical. She entered trauma therapy. Learned breathwork. Attended a grief circle for doctors.

Outcome:

She now leads monthly emotional processing sessions in hospitals. Doctors cry without shame. Nurses share without fear.

"We became better healers when we stopped pretending, we were unbreakable."

◆ 15.6 The Social Side of Resilience

Humans are **wired for co-regulation.**

"We heal faster in safe company than in solitary silence."

Resilience Boosters:

- Empathic listening
- Safe, nonjudgmental friendships
- Mentorship and community belonging
- Witnessing others' comebacks

📌 **Social Case Study:**

Dinesh, a high-school principal, implemented peer resilience circles for teacher's post-pandemic.

Burnout dropped by 37%. Teachers said:

"I've never felt so seen while struggling."

◆ 15.7 Resilience in the Face of Repeated Trauma

Some people aren't recovering from **one event** – but from **years of compounded pain.**

This is called **Complex Trauma** – and resilience looks different here.

For Complex Trauma:

- Healing is **non-linear.**
- Relapses are expected.
- Micro-wins matter.

- Support must be specialized (trauma-informed therapy, EMDR, somatic tools)

🎙 **Anecdote:**

Shalini, a survivor of childhood neglect and partner violence, said:

"I don't bounce back – I rebuild. Slowly. Safely. And I don't do it alone anymore."

That's resilience – without the toxic positivity.

◆ 15.8 How to Train for Resilience Like a Muscle

"If resilience is a muscle – how are you training it?"

Daily Practices:

- ✍ Reflective journaling: "What hurt me today – and what did it teach?"
- 🧘 Breathwork to soothe stress response
- 🧠 Reframing exercises (What's a new way to see this?)
- Self-forgiveness practices
- 💬 Asking for help without apology

Weekly Habits:

- Celebrate micro-wins.
- Unplug from emotional triggers.
- Spend time with someone safe.
- Do something that affirms your identity beyond your pain.

◆ 15.9 Resilient Leadership: Teaching Others How to Rise

"When a leader owns their scars, the whole room heals."

Resilient leaders:

- Normalize setbacks.

- Praise effort, not outcome.
- Share personal stories of overcoming.
- Create psychological safety.
- Protect rest – not just performance.

📌 **Organizational Case Study:**

Zara Tech, a design company, implemented failure showcases.

Every month, a team member shares what went wrong – and what they learned.

Innovation rose by 62% in 6 months.

"Resilience became culture – not just crisis response."

◆ **Case Study 1:** ***"Ritika and the Burnout Illusion"***

Ritika, a brilliant 27-year-old product designer in Bangalore, was everyone's favourite success story – until the burnout came. On the outside, she was the perfect example of resilience: late-night hustler, never missed a deadline, always smiled through adversity. But inside, she was unravelling.

"I called it resilience, but I was just white knuckling through trauma. I didn't know the difference."

The real turning point came one evening when she fainted in the middle of a presentation. The hospital report read: exhaustion, anxiety-induced vertigo, and emotional fatigue.

Her therapist helped her redefine resilience:

- Not pushing through, but **listening inward**
- Not showing strength, but **honouring vulnerability**
- Not always bouncing back, but **slowly rising forward**

Today, Ritika leads workshops titled *"Recovery is Resilience"* and coaches startup founders on **ethical endurance** – showing them how emotional clarity sustains innovation more than constant hustle.

◆ Case Study 2: *"Arun's Redirection"*

At 48, Arun was the regional head of a multinational, until a "sudden restructuring" cost him his job.

He spiralled.

"My job was my identity. Losing it felt like dying."

For weeks, he isolated himself. He stopped shaving. Avoided calls. Then one day, while sorting through old papers, he found an idea journal from his college days – full of consultancy frameworks, branding models, and leadership hacks.

He wept.

"I remembered the version of me that existed before titles. That kid had ideas. That kid mattered."

He dusted off the journal, rewrote his mission, and began consulting. Slowly, clients returned. His first big contract? The very company that fired him.

Now, Arun teaches "*Resilience as Reinvention*" in business schools and says:

"You don't always bounce back into the same box. Sometimes, you bounce back into your real calling."

◆ Case Study 3: *"Janice and the Coffee Breakdown"*

Janice was a celebrated paediatrician with two Ivy League degrees. Everyone called her "the strong one."

But one morning, her coffee spilled on her favourite blouse before a conference. She fell to the floor and sobbed for twenty minutes. It wasn't the coffee.

"It was everything I had held back for twenty years – pouring out through that one stain."

Her therapist later said:

"Janice, you were never weak. You were emotionally constipated."

That crack became her liberation. She began therapy, started painting again, and even took a sabbatical to train as a trauma-informed medical leader.

Today, she says:

"My breakdown was my breakthrough. I stopped pretending strength – and started practicing softness."

◆ Case Study 4: *"Dinesh's Teacher Resilience Circle"*

As the pandemic tore through systems, Dinesh – a compassionate principal from Pune – watched his faculty disintegrate emotionally.

"They were breaking, but they kept showing up. That's not noble. That's dangerous."

He initiated a radical concept: **Resilience Circles** – small, weekly gatherings where teachers could cry, talk, rest, and recover in community.

Each circle opened with:

"You're not here to be strong. You're here to be seen."

Over the next six months:

- Teacher absences dropped.
- Conflicts decreased.
- Creative lesson plans surged.

One teacher wrote:

"I used to go home with everyone's trauma. Now I leave with a piece of my soul still intact."

◆ Case Study 5: *"Shalini's Complex Comeback"*

Shalini, 36, was a survivor of childhood emotional neglect, narcissistic abuse, and an abusive first marriage. By the time she reached therapy, she said:

"I'm not even a person anymore. I'm just reactions."

Resilience for her didn't look like bouncing back.

It looked like:

- Trusting one friend with one secret
- Taking one hour a week without guilt
- Buying clothes that felt soft instead of flattering.
- Saying "no" without a trembling voice

Her therapist called these "micro-wins."

They called it "progress."

Shalini called it: *"reclaiming my soul inch by inch."*

Now she's a peer mentor for trauma survivors and speaks publicly about **complex resilience**:

"Don't ask people to bounce back when they've never even known safe ground. Sometimes, healing is learning how to just stand."

◆ Case Study 6: *"Zara Tech's Resilience Revolution"*

Zara Tech, a design innovation firm, struggled post-recession. Productivity dipped. Morale was gone. Their CEO, a firm believer in vulnerability-based leadership, tried something bold.

He introduced:

- **Failure Forums** (where team members shared the flops and the funny)
- **Gratitude Walls**
- **Resilience Pods** (for meditation, journaling, and peer support)

Each new hire was given a resilience toolkit on Day One – including an emotional check-in wheel, journal, and a personal coach.

"Our people were brilliant. They just needed permission to break – and space to rebuild."

The result?

- Product launches doubled.
- Innovation time rose by 52%.
- Turnover dropped by 40%.

Zara Tech's new motto?

"We don't just build things. We rebuild people."

◆ Closing Reflection

These case studies reveal a critical truth:

Resilience is not a destination.

It's not a personality type.

It's not a single bounce.

It's a **practice**, a **process**, and most of all – a **permission** to honour your pain and still move forward.

Every reader, whether a **psychologist, leader, teacher, parent, healer, or seeker**, must remember:

Resilience doesn't ask you to erase your story.

It asks you to **rewrite how it ends**.

📌 Chapter 15 Summary – The Art of Becoming Unbreakable

"Resilience doesn't mean you never bend. It means you know how to **rise differently**."

~ Anonymous

You are not the failure.

You are not the fear.

You are not the story someone else wrote.

You are:

- The rewrite
- The comeback
- The breath between chaos and clarity

Resilience is not about getting back to who you were.

It's about becoming who you're meant to be.

And that journey – is yours to own.

Chapter 16: The Anatomy of Self-Betrayal — How to Stop Abandoning Your Inner Truth

"Every time you swallow your truth to keep the peace, you start a war inside yourself."

~ Anonymous

◆ 16.1 What Is Self-Betrayal?

Self-betrayal is not always loud.

It's often silent.

Insidious.

Sanitized as "being nice," "doing the right thing," or "not making a scene."

But what it really is — is this:

- Saying yes when your soul is screaming no.
- Laughing when you're hurting.
- Shrinking your needs to fit someone else's comfort.

Self-betrayal is the chronic, subtle, and sometimes violent habit of **choosing others over yourself** — not out of love, but out of fear.

◆ 16.2 The Origins of Self-Betrayal

No child wakes up thinking, "I'll betray myself to survive."

But when:

- Crying gets you ignored.
- Anger gets you punished.

- Being different gets you mocked
- You learn to adapt.

You learn:

"I'll be who you want me to be – so you'll stay, so I'll be safe."

This is the birth of **emotional shape-shifting.**

You become who others need, at the cost of who you are.

🔍 **Anecdote:**

Rina, now 34, spent her entire childhood being the "perfect daughter."

Straight A's. Polite. Obedient.

"I was everyone's pride – and my own prison."

"When I finally had a panic attack in a grocery store, I realized: I don't know who I am. I only know who I was taught to be."

◆ 16.3 The Five Faces of Self-Betrayal

Self-betrayal wears masks – often praised by society.

🩹 1. The People-Pleaser

You say what they want to hear. You over-extend. You perform kindness at the cost of authenticity.

"If I disappoint them, I lose love."

But the truth is:

"If love requires performance, it's not love. It's leverage."

🔒 2. The Silence Keeper

You don't speak up when something feels wrong. You tolerate microaggressions. You bury truths.

"I don't want conflict."

But silence is not peace – it's paralysis.

🛑 3. The Chronic Apologizer

You say sorry when you're not sorry. You shrink after expressing a need. You second-guess yourself into emotional invisibility.

🎭 4. The Mask-Wearer

You wear confidence like armour. You laugh loudly to hide the tremble in your voice. You're never really "in the room" because you've left your truth at the door.

🚶 5. The Self-Abandoner

You ghost your own dreams. You stay in places that poison your soul.

"Maybe I'm just too much."

No. Maybe **they're not enough to hold your fire.**

◆ 16.4 The Cost of Self-Betrayal

Every unspoken truth stack inside you like a slow bomb.

It doesn't go away. It **waits.**

Symptoms of long-term self-betrayal:

- Chronic fatigue
- Identity confusion
- Passive-aggression
- Depression masked as politeness.
- Anxiety attacks when "nothing is wrong".

📌 Case Study:

Dev, a corporate executive, followed all the rules – Ivy League, perfect marriage, six-figure salary.

One day, he walked into his office, looked around, and thought:

"None of this is mine. I built a life based on expectations, not authenticity."

He left. Not impulsively – but intentionally.

Now, he's a mental health advocate.

"Success is suffocating when it's built on self-abandonment."

◆ 16.5 Why We Keep Doing It (Even When We Know Better)

Because self-betrayal is safe. Familiar.

You think:

- "If I speak up, they'll leave."
- "If I show up fully, I'll be judged."
- "If I slow down, I'll lose everything."

These fears come from **relational trauma** – moments when being real **cost you connection.**

So now, you associate truth with punishment.

But your truth is **not the problem.**

Their inability to hold it was.

◆ 16.6 How to Reclaim Your Inner Truth

🔥 Step 1: Recognize the Pattern

Ask:

"Where am I pretending?"

"What truth am I choking back?"

🛠 Step 2: Rehearse Truth in Safe Spaces

Truth is a **muscle.** Don't flex it first in warzones.

Practice saying what you really mean to people who won't punish you for it.

🖍 Step 3: Grieve the Mask

Let yourself feel the sadness, rage, or numbness that comes with decades of hiding.

You're not broken – you're unthawing.

🌱 Step 4: Choose Micro-Honesty Daily

Say:

- "I don't want to do that."
- "That doesn't feel right."
- "I disagree – respectfully."
- "No, thank you."

You don't need to yell to be heard.

You just need to **stop erasing yourself.**

◆ 16.7 From Betrayal to Belonging – Without Performing

You're allowed to be:

- Flawed and still worthy.
- Messy and still loveable
- Honest and still held.

📌 Real-Life Recovery:

Fatima, 42, left an emotionally toxic marriage after 18 years.

"I was dying in silence. And no one knew – because I made it look beautiful."

Now, she facilitates workshops on emotional sovereignty.

Her mantra: "Peace is expensive when it costs your truth. I'm done paying."

📌 Chapter 16 Summary — The Reckoning and the Return

"You don't lose people when you speak your truth. You lose illusions. And illusions were never your people anyway."

– Anonymous

Self-betrayal may have helped you survive.

But **you're not surviving anymore. You're awakening.**

And awakening means:

- No more masks
- No more shrinking
- No more starving yourself of your own voice

This chapter is your permission slip to **come home to yourself.**

Loudly. Softly. Fiercely. Finally.

Chapter 17: The Art of Self-Forgiveness — Making Peace with the Person in the Mirror

"You can't truly begin again until you stop bleeding over who you used to be."

~ Anonymous

🧭 Chapter 17: Healing Emotional Baggage — Understanding the Weight We Carry and How to Let It Go

"We all carry bags — some filled with grief, some with guilt, some with silence. Healing begins the moment we unzip them, look inside, and say: I see you. I'm ready to let go."

~ Anonymous

◆ 17.1 What Is Self-Forgiveness, Really?

Self-forgiveness isn't a spiritual meme.

It's **emotional surgery**.

It's peeling off shame like dead skin — piece by piece — until you can finally breathe again.

It's not saying:

- "What I did was okay."
- But rather:
- "I am not only what I did."

Self-forgiveness is the **bold act of unchaining yourself from past decisions, mistakes, and versions** of who you once were.

It asks you to:

- Face your past without flinching.
- Feel your remorse without drowning.
- Learn without looping in shame.

📍**Anecdote:**

Devika, a 36-year-old former addict, once told her support group:

"I kept saying sorry to everyone – but never to the little girl inside me who was screaming for help all those years."

When she finally forgave herself, she stopped sabotaging her healing.

She wrote herself a letter:

"I forgive you for not knowing better. You do now. That's enough."

And that became her liberation.

◆ 17.2 The Layers of Self-Forgiveness

Self-forgiveness isn't a one-step decision. It's a **multi-layered grief ritual:**

1. Guilt – "I did something wrong."

This is healthy. Guilt invites repair.

2. Shame – "I *am* something wrong."

This is toxic. It becomes your identity if unchecked.

3. Regret – "If I could go back..."

Common. But dangerous when it hijacks the present.

4. Rumination – "Why did I do that?"

An emotional loop that paralyzes progress.

5. Release – "I'm not that moment anymore."

Freedom. But not forgetting – evolving.

"Forgiveness doesn't erase your past – it stops it from erasing you."

◆ 17.3 Real Case Studies of People Who Forgave Themselves

💔 Case 1: The Father Who Cheated

Ravi, 41, cheated on his wife. He confessed. She left. His kids stopped talking to him.

For two years, he wore his shame like a skin suit.

He said:

"I knew I hurt them. But I started believing I didn't deserve love. That belief made me hurt others again."

Therapy helped him reframe:

- He wasn't *just* the affair.
- He was a human who broke – and chose to heal.
- He began to volunteer, mentor young fathers, and write letters of amends (even if not returned)

"I can't change the past. But I can stop dragging it through every tomorrow."

💔 Case 2: The Daughter Who Ghosted

Meena, 29, cut ties with her mom during her rebellious twenties.

Her mother died unexpectedly. Meena spiralled.

She told her counsellor:

"I didn't even say goodbye. I was angry. Now I feel like a monster."

Her healing began not in denial – but in grief.

She wrote to her late mother every week for a year.

She hosted a women's circle about generational trauma.

She became the mother to herself that she never had.

"I will never erase what I didn't say. But I won't let silence be my legacy."

💔 Case 3: The Healer Who Burned Out

Ishaan, a therapist, prided himself on being strong. He took on suicidal clients without proper supervision. One of them took his life.

He shut down.

Stopped practicing.

Spiralled into self-blame.

In group therapy, someone said:

"You were never meant to be a god. Just a guide."

That sentence saved his practice – and his soul.

He returned to therapy, this time with boundaries.

He now trains new therapists on *safety and humility.*

"I forgave myself not because I didn't fail – but because I finally understood how to fail forward."

◆ 17.4 What Self-Forgiveness Is NOT

- It's NOT bypassing consequences.
- It's NOT spiritual arrogance.
- It's NOT instant.

It is:

- Owning the full weight of your actions
- Making amends where possible
- Grieving the version of yourself that didn't know better.
- Creating a new legacy from the lesson

"You can't punish yourself into healing."

◆ 17.5 The Psychology of Self-Forgiveness

Psychologists define self-forgiveness as a **four-stage process:**

1. **Responsibility** – Admit without deflection.
2. **Remorse** – Feel without self-destruction.
3. **Repair** – Apologize (internally or externally)
4. **Renewal** – Commit to different actions.

Insight:

People who struggle with self-forgiveness often have:

- Authoritarian childhoods
- Perfectionistic belief systems
- Shame-based identities

Healing tip: Replace the inner critic with the inner nurturer.

◆ 17.6 Self-Forgiveness and Relationships

Unforgiven guilt seeps into:

- Passive-aggression
- Overcompensation
- Sabotaging intimacy
- People-pleasing or stonewalling

Story:

Arjun, who couldn't forgive himself for abandoning his ex during her depression, now sabotages every new relationship.

His therapist asked:

"What if being loved now doesn't mean your past is erased — just that you're ready to be different?"

That was the crack where the light got in.

17.7 – The Hidden Price of Pretending: When Adaptation Becomes Self-Betrayal

"The mask you wear to survive can suffocate the person you were born to be."

~ Anonymous

There comes a point in life where many people don't just lose touch with their dreams. They lose touch with their truth.

Not because they're weak.

Not because they're dishonest.

But because survival demanded a version of them that could **fit** – in a family, in a relationship, in a culture, in a career.

That's the dangerous magic of **adaptation**.

It looks like resilience.

But sometimes, it's self-erasure.

The Quiet Erosion of Authenticity

Every time you swallow your truth to keep peace, or force a smile to maintain an image, or agree when you're screaming inside – **you chip away at your centre**.

People call this maturity. Society calls it professionalism.

But at its worst, it's a betrayal of self that leaves emotional residue like:

- unexplained exhaustion
- chronic resentment
- a sense that "something is missing".
- numbness even in joyful moments

🎭 Case Study 1: The Empathic Executive Who Lost Herself

Radhika, 39, was a rising star at a global tech firm.

Outwardly confident. Internally crumbling. She'd become an expert in **emotional shape-shifting** – absorbing everyone's stress, fixing every broken process, and saying yes until her calendar bled red.

In therapy, she confessed:

"I'm the person everyone depends on – but I don't know who I am anymore."

She didn't need a promotion. She needed permission – to **drop the mask**, to **say no without shame**, to choose herself without guilt.

The breakthrough came when she stopped asking, "What will they think?"

And started asking, "What do I need?"

💔 Case Study 2: The Mother Who Forgot to Be a Woman

Neena, a 46-year-old mother of three, spent decades meeting the needs of others.

Her husband. Her in-laws. Her children. Her community.

She hadn't bought clothes for herself in five years.

She hadn't cried in even longer.

"I forgot how to want something that was just for me," she whispered in a women's circle.

"I love my family, but I don't know who I am outside of them."

She wasn't depressed.

She was disembodied – **living so externally**, she'd left her inner life behind.

Her healing started not with therapy – but with **solitude**. A locked room. A journal. 20 minutes of uninterrupted "Neena time."

She found that she didn't need to escape her life.

She just needed to **reclaim space** in it.

🤐 Case Study 3: The Silent Son

Amit, 27, grew up in a home where emotions were liabilities.

His father called crying "drama." His mother smiled through pain.

By the time Amit reached adulthood, he couldn't identify what he felt.

Joy, grief, love – they were all buried under a script of compliance:

"Be strong. Be quiet. Be what they expect."

When his long-term girlfriend left him, her parting words pierced deeper than the breakup:

"I never knew what was real with you."

Amit didn't need fixing. He needed **permission to feel.**

He began seeing a somatic therapist who said:

"Your body remembers everything your mouth never said."

His voice, once muted by shame, now shakes – but **it speaks.**

🔒 Case Study 4: The Coach Who Couldn't Coach Herself

Leena, a mindset coach, built a brand teaching self-love.

But behind closed doors, she couldn't say no to her emotionally manipulative partner.

He belittled her. Took credit for her ideas. Controlled her finances subtly.

"I help people honour themselves, but I let myself get erased."

The irony wasn't lost on her.

And that's the **paradox of emotional labour** – the more you give to others, the easier it is to forget to protect yourself.

Her recovery was radical.

She fired clients who drained her.

She downsized her life.

She found a therapist who said:

"You're not here to save everyone. You're here to **be** someone."

Why We Betray Ourselves

Self-betrayal doesn't begin as a conscious act. It begins as a **protective mechanism.**

We betray ourselves when:

- Love feels conditional.
- Belonging depends on silence.
- Identity is shaped by fear.
- The world punishes truth-tellers.

"Fitting in" becomes more important than feeling whole.

But the cost of that adaptation?

A life that looks full – but feels empty.

A version of you that everyone loves – except you.

What Healing Looks Like

Healing from self-betrayal isn't about self-improvement.

It's about **self-return.**

You don't need a 5-step plan.

You need:

- A **mirror** that doesn't lie
- A **safe space** where you don't have to perform.
- And a **ritual** of coming home to your body, your truth, your voice.

🧘 Reader Reflection Prompts

1. What part of me have I been hiding to keep others comfortable?
2. When did I first learn that my truth was "too much"?
3. Who do I become when I don't feel safe to be real?
4. What truth have I abandoned – and what would it cost to reclaim it?

"The cost of pretending is your peace.

The cost of silence is your soul.

The cost of self-betrayal is a life unlived."

-- Anonymous

You don't have to keep paying that price.

Come back to you.

Piece by piece.

Truth by truth.

Breath by breath.

📌 Chapter 17 Summary – Your Past Is Not Your Prison

"You are allowed to be the person who did the wrong thing – and also the person who learned, wept, and rose anyway."

-- Anonymous

You are not:

- Your lowest moment
- Your worst decision
- Your last failure

You are:

- Every brave choice to heal anyway.

- Every sleepless night where you chose reflection over running.
- Every "I forgive you" whispered into the mirror.

And that – that is how you begin again.

Chapter 18: Perspectives: The two different foundation scenarios.

Part I: "Beyond the Grades: The Psychological Toll of Parental Expectations on Children's Mental Health"

The Psychological Framework – How Parental Expectations Shape Mental Health

1.0 Introduction: A Culture of Pressure

"Children are not things to be moulded, but people to be unfolded." - Jess Lair

In a world increasingly obsessed with metrics – grades, achievements, trophies – we have unconsciously built an emotional guillotine suspended over the heads of our youth. The tender minds of children, born with curiosity and a desire for love, now often bloom under conditions more akin to a performance lab than a nurturing garden.

Parental expectations, once rooted in care and ambition, have in many cultures and family systems, evolved into perfectionist scripts written for children to act out, often at the expense of their own mental well-being. This pressure has far-reaching implications – chronic stress, anxiety, depression, identity confusion, and a haunting sense of "not being enough."

This essay explores how these expectations – often unspoken yet deeply internalized – affect the psychological makeup of a child, backed by developmental psychology, modern clinical studies, and poignant real-life accounts.

2.0 The Anatomy of Parental Expectations

2.1 Origins of the Expectation Epidemic

- Societal glorification of "success stories"
- Intergenerational trauma: Parents projecting their unrealized dreams onto children.
- Media-fed comparisons and cultural prestige linked to academic success.

2.2 Healthy vs. Toxic Expectations

Not all expectations are harmful. The line is drawn where love becomes conditional — praise is only given when goals are met. Healthy encouragement fosters resilience; toxic ambition cultivates insecurity.

Healthy Expectation Traits:

- Open dialogue
- Emphasis on effort, not just outcome
- Recognition of individual strengths

Toxic Expectation Traits:

- Conditional love or approval
- Emphasis on comparison and performance
- Rejection of failures or alternative interests

3.0 Mental Health Ramifications of High Expectations

"Behind every young child who believes in themselves is a parent who believed first." - Matthew L. Jacobson

3.1 Chronic Stress and Cortisol Overload

Studies show that children under constant performance pressure have elevated cortisol levels — leading to insomnia, fatigue, panic attacks, and impaired memory formation.

3.2 Identity Suppression

When a child grows up chasing a life not of their choosing, they disconnect from their authentic self. This often results in:

- Suppressed desires.
- Poor emotional vocabulary
- Difficulty in relationships and decision-making in adulthood

3.3 Anxiety and Depression

- 43% of adolescents with overly critical parents show signs of clinical anxiety.
- The dread of "not measuring up" manifests in social withdrawal, mood swings, and learned helplessness.

4.0 The Cultural Context: East vs. West

4.1 Collectivist Cultures (e.g., India, China)

Success equates to family honour. Children are seen as extensions of their parents' legacies, leading to:

- High pressure for academic perfection
- Stigma around emotional expression
- Career paths pre-determined by family expectation

4.2 Individualist Cultures (e.g., USA, UK)

While encouraging freedom, these cultures often harbour:

- Competitive school environments
- High social media-driven comparison
- Pressure to stand out as "unique" and "gifted".

In both frameworks, the common denominator remains: a child's worth is increasingly externalized.

5.0 Generational Cycles and Internalized Pressure

"If we don't heal what hurt us, we'll bleed on those who didn't cut us." – Unknown

5.1 The Cycle of Control

Children under controlling parents may grow into controlling adults – replicating the same pressure they resented. Without intervention, the cycle continues.

5.2 The "Good Child Syndrome"

This refers to children who strive to be perfect to avoid parental disappointment, developing:

- People-pleasing behaviours
- Difficulty asserting boundaries.
- Deep fears of rejection

6.0 Redefining Success: Breaking the Cycle

Success must be redefined from grades and gold medals to:

- Emotional resilience
- Healthy relationships
- Inner peace and purpose

Recommendations:

- Teach emotional intelligence at home.
- Replace "Why didn't you get full marks?" with "What did you enjoy learning?"
- Encourage hobbies that don't lead to awards.

Case Studies and Real-Life Accounts

"The scars they carry aren't visible on their report cards."

Chapter Title: **The Price of Perfection — How Parental Expectations Wound the Soul**

This section will unfold in four major parts:

1. **The Psychological Battlefield** - Deep dive into emotional damage caused by high parental expectations.
2. **Childhood Interrupted** - Real-life reflections and character-driven analysis.
3. **From Expectations to Exile** - Identity, disconnection, and long-term trauma
4. **Healing the Fracture** - Resilience, recovery, and rewriting the script
5. **Short Story** - *"The Trophy Wall"* — a hauntingly beautiful, fictionalized narrative that captures the lived truth of so many.

🧨 SECTION 1: THE PSYCHOLOGICAL BATTLEFIELD

Where Report Cards Replace Relationships, and Performance Becomes Identity

"He got 95 and still came home scared."

🧠 1.1 THE INVISIBLE WAR IN HOUSEHOLDS

Every day, behind closed doors that look picture-perfect from the outside, children wage a silent war. A war not fought with fists or weapons — but with **report cards, silence, shame, and expectations.**

The battlefield? Their mind.

The enemy? Not their parents — but **the belief that love must be earned.**

This is the hidden emotional architecture of millions of families:

- "Score well, or you're lazy."

- "Be first, or you're failing."
- "Win the gold, or don't bother coming home."

The child doesn't resist – they *absorb*.

They start believing:

"If I don't perform, I don't belong."

They internalize this:

- Worth = marks
- Identity = success
- Safety = obedience
- Love = conditional

And when this continues unchecked?

It breaks the child from within – long before adulthood.

💧 1.2 THE TRAUMA OF 'NOT ENOUGH'

The trauma of high parental expectations is **not always physical** – it's psychological, emotional, and spiritual.

It comes in whispers:

- "You could've done better."
- "Look at Sharmaji's son."
- "Why did you get 92 instead of 95?"
- "Don't embarrass us."
- "Failure is not an option."

Children raised in this climate don't grow up feeling empowered.

They grow up **afraid of rest, rejection, and reflection.**

They live in constant hypervigilance:

- "What if I don't top?"
- "What if I fail?"

- "What if I lose them?"

This leads to:

- High-functioning anxiety
- Self-worth tied only to achievement.
- Emotional suppression
- Academic burnout
- Depression masked as discipline.
- Suicide ideation in severe cases.

🔍Case Fragment – *From Your Document:*

"I was never allowed to say I was tired. I had to smile after every medal, not because I was proud – but because I was scared what would happen if I didn't bring one home."

That child, anonymous in the study, went on to **avoid praise**, **distrust success**, and **fear joy** – because their nervous system associated all of it with **pressure**.

This is what emotional trauma looks like in gifted children.

💣 1.3 THE CRUSHING COST OF EXPECTATIONAL ABUSE

Let's call it what it is:

When children are not allowed to fail, rest, question, cry, or define their own dreams – it is **emotional abuse dressed as ambition.**

And it comes from **love without emotional intelligence.**

"I only want the best for you" – they say.

But if the "best" comes with fear, anxiety, pressure, panic, insomnia, and suicidal thoughts... is it really love?

💥 **Case Expansion:**

Rohan, 16, was forced into coaching for IIT at 13.

- Weekly schedule: 6 AM study, 8 hours school, 4 hours coaching, no social life.
- Topper in class but constantly had stomach ulcers.
- Tried to end his life when his rank dropped from AIR 40 to 118

Therapist's notes:

"Rohan didn't want to die. He wanted the pressure to stop. But he didn't know how to ask for it – because asking meant 'weakness.'"

Today, Rohan is alive. But he still can't enjoy achievement. Every success feels like a **trigger** for the next war.

🧨 1.4 THE PSYCHOLOGICAL FORMULA OF PARENTAL DAMAGE

Let's break this down into a formula:

[Love + Expectations] – Emotional Safety = Internalized Shame

Children raised like this:

- Learn to perform, not express.
- Learn to hide, not heal.
- Learn to achieve, not ask.
- Learn to fake happiness, not feel truth.

The nervous system becomes **hyper-regulated**, always on edge, waiting for the next "why not 100?" moment.

They don't play.

They don't rest.

They don't dream.

They survive.

⚠ 1.5 LONG-TERM EFFECTS ON ADULT LIFE

The most successful people on paper?

Many of them are **still recovering from childhood**.

Years later, the scars show up as:

- Workaholism
- Inability to enjoy rest without guilt.
- Perfectionism
- Emotional numbness
- Fear of relationships
- Panic around failure.
- Imposter syndrome despite achievements

📌 **Case – From the Corporate World:**

Meera, 34, an Ivy League graduate and VP at a fintech startup, came to therapy because she had **daily panic attacks despite "having it all."**

Therapist asked: "When do you feel most unsafe?"

She answered:

"When someone praises me. Because I know I'll have to top that again."

Her father only hugged her after trophies.

Today, she can't feel **unconditional joy**.

🧠 1.6 A CULTURE THAT NEEDS TO PAUSE

This isn't just about individual parents.

It's a **cultural epidemic.**

We worship outcomes.

We shame softness.

We compare children like products.

And in doing so, we're raising **emotionally brilliant kids who are spiritually hollow.**

It must stop.

We must ask:

What's the cost of an 'A+' if it comes with anxiety, addiction, and abandonment?

🛠 1.7 THE PSYCHOLOGICAL BATTLEFIELD – KEY INSIGHTS

- **Not all trauma is loud.** Sometimes it's silence, perfection, and pressure.
- **Not all gifted kids are okay.** Some are silently breaking down.
- **Parents mean well.** But love without listening is still dangerous.
- **The human behind the grade matters more than the grade.**
- **If children must break themselves to be accepted — it is not parenting. It is oppression.**

SECTION 2: CHILDHOOD INTERRUPTED

Where joy is postponed, identity is hijacked, and silence becomes survival.

"I was never a child. I was a project."

2.1 CASE FILE: AARAV, THE SMILING CHAMELEON

Age at breakdown: 17

Condition: Panic attacks, self-harm

Parental profile: Father - retired Colonel, Mother - school principal

Surface status: All-India academic topper, fluent in five languages, national level quizzer

Reality: Hadn't slept properly in 18 months.

📖 HIS STORY

Aarav was the definition of *ideal.*

Polished. Polite. Perfect.

Until the day he collapsed in the school washroom after a debate competition.

Blood on his shirt from scratching his own chest in panic.

Hyperventilation. Crying. Shaking.

When asked what triggered him, he said:

"I didn't win best speaker... my fathers in the audience... I don't know how to face him."

He didn't cry about losing.

He cried about *not being good enough for his father's pride.*

That wasn't the first time.

That was just the first time **he broke in public.**

In private, he'd been breaking for years.

🧠 Psychological Analysis:

- Aarav had **perfect child syndrome**
- Every achievement was met with, "Good. What's next?"
- He learned to perform emotions – not feel them
- His identity was **a reflection of parental pride**, not personal desire

🔥 Key Reflection:

He once told his counsellor:

"I'm not living a life – I'm maintaining an illusion that makes them love me."

Aarav is healing now. Slowly. With therapy, music, and finally – **imperfection.**

🌧 2.2 CASE FILE: SANJANA, THE GOLDEN GIRL WHO CRUMBLED

Age at collapse: 15

Symptoms: Suicidal ideation, eating disorder

Parental backdrop: Single mother, academic legacy

Surface image: Dancer, head girl, Math Olympiad winner

Hidden wound: Couldn't eat without guilt

📖 HER STORY

Sanjana's mother was her idol – a professor, a widow, a woman of discipline.

So when her mother said:

"No one will love a lazy girl,"

Sanjana believed her.

She stopped eating carbs.

She ran 7 km every day.

She stopped smiling in pictures.

And she fainted during school rehearsals.

Not because of stress.

Because of **starvation, silence, and shame.**

💔 One Journal Entry:

"If I fail, she won't say anything. That's how I'll know she's disappointed."

Sanjana didn't need her mother to push harder.

She needed someone to say:

"You can rest. You're already enough."

That sentence came too late.

But recovery started when she wrote it to *herself*.

2.3 CASE FILE: ARJUN & THE INVISIBLE BOY

Age at freeze: 11

Presenting issue: Selective mutism, trust deficits

Parental culture: Dual income, high-pressure, tech entrepreneurs

Home rule: "No excuses. Only results."

His rebellion: Silence

HIS STORY

Arjun was not defiant.

He was invisible.

In school, he stopped speaking to teachers.

Not because he had speech issues.

But because speaking **never earned him love at home.**

His father gave him feedback like a CEO.

His mother outsourced affection to tutors, therapists, and schedules.

Arjun's therapist said:

"He didn't need structure. He needed affection."

When asked why he won't speak in class, Arjun said:

"No one listens anyway. They just wait for me to finish so they can grade me."

Observation:

Arjun is not disobedient.

He's traumatized by **chronic emotional neglect dressed as discipline.**

2.4 CASE FILE: PRIYA, THE GHOST IN A PERFECT BODY

Age at rupture: 19

Issues: Dissociation, sexual anxiety, panic in intimacy

Family: High-achieving academic family, deeply patriarchal

Surface: Medical student, always composed

Secret: Lived in complete emotional dissociation from her body

HER STORY

Priya was never asked how she felt.

Only how she ranked.

When she once cried before her NEET mock test, her father slapped her and said:

"You don't have time to be weak. Be a warrior."

She stopped crying after that.

She also stopped feeling.

Years later, when she entered her first romantic relationship, she panicked.

Not because of her partner.

Because **touch triggered trauma.**

Affection triggered fear.

Her body didn't know safety.

Her mind only knew survival.

2.5 WHAT THESE CASES TEACH US

- Parental pride without presence equals **emotional abandonment**
- High-achievers are often **highly anxious**
- Emotional starvation is as dangerous as physical abuse

- "I just want the best for you" can sound like "you are not enough as you are"
- **Love is not love when it requires perfection to be accessed**

⚡ CLOSING THIS SECTION: CHILDHOOD INTERRUPTED

We must ask ourselves:

How many doctors, CEOs, engineers, and gold medallists are walking around as **wounded children in adult suits?**

How many of them were never allowed to say:

"I'm tired. I'm scared. I'm confused. I don't want this."

And how many parents are still confusing **achievement with love**?

SECTION 3: FROM EXPECTATIONS TO EXILE

The Disconnection from Self Begins Here

"At some point, I stopped asking what I wanted. I only cared about what would make them proud."

🧠 3.1 WHEN PERFORMANCE REPLACES PERSONHOOD

Children under chronic pressure don't grow with love.

They grow with **compliance**.

They don't ask, "Who am I?" – they ask, "What do I need to become so they'll approve?"

They become:

- Obedient robots
- Hyper-adaptive chameleons
- Anxious achievers

And they start **exiling their true selves:**

- Hobbies get dropped.

- Desires get silenced.
- Play turns into productivity.
- Curiosity turns into compliance.

Eventually, **they don't know who they are** beyond grades, medals, and performance.

💧 3.2 CASE FILE: KARAN, THE LOST SON WITH A PERFECT RESUME

Age at realization: 21

Background: IIT graduate, placed in FAANG

Presenting problem: Identity crisis, disassociation, panic during success

Real wound: "I never got to choose my own life."

📖 HIS STORY

Karan had done everything "right."

Top university. Dream job. Massive package.

But inside?

"Every time someone congratulates me, I feel like I'm disappearing."

He didn't feel *seen* – he felt **performed.**

In therapy, Karan admitted:

"I don't remember ever saying no to my parents. Not once."

His dreams weren't his. His wins weren't his.

And when he sat alone in his new apartment, he sobbed.

Because he didn't know what he loved. Or who he was without deadlines.

That's **exile**: when your life is built so far from your truth, even success feels like suffocation.

🌪 3.3 THE IDENTITY FRACTURE

"What happens to a child who is taught to be everything but themselves?"

They fragment.

They split into:

- Public face (performer)
- Private ache (the repressed child)
- Future fear (the adult who doesn't know who they are)

They become **highly competent but emotionally hollow.**

Smart but self-sabotaging.

Loved but never safe.

🍬 3.4 THE PSYCHOLOGY OF SELF-ERASURE

Children who learn they must please others to be accepted stop asking, "What do I want?"

They instead ask:

- "What should I want?"
- "What will make them proud?"
- "What will get me noticed?"

This leads to:

- Chronic indecision
- Suppressed anger
- Identity foreclosure
- Relationship dysfunction
- Body dissociation (especially in girls)

📌 **Research Integration:**

Studies reveal that children subjected to **constant parental expectations** begin to **internalize achievement as their only value marker**. This leads to:

- A fragile ego structure
- Over-identification with performance roles
- Panic in rest
- High rates of burnout and perfectionism in adulthood

🌊 3.5 THE COST OF CULTURAL SHAME

In collectivist cultures (like much of South Asia), identity is often defined by **family honour**, **academic excellence**, and **social compliance.**

Children don't ask "what's my dream?"

They're taught: "Your dream is our dream."

And when they rebel, they face:

- Emotional withdrawal
- Public shaming
- Comparisons to siblings or peers
- Dismissal of personal interests

💥 **Case Example:**

Fatima, 19, wanted to study literature.

Her family said, "Writers are losers. Be a doctor."

She obeyed. But every time she touched a stethoscope, she wanted to scream.

One night, she carved the word "TRAPPED" into her arm.

Today, she's studying creative writing. Her scars are fading. But her trust in love that doesn't control her? Still in recovery.

🧨 3.6 EXILE DOESN'T JUST HAPPEN – IT'S TAUGHT

It starts early:

- "Stop crying – it's weak."
- "Maths is more important than music."
- "Topper's parents don't complain."
- "Get serious – dreams don't pay the bills."

So children **dismantle their own joy.**

They exile:

- Their art
- Their sensitivity
- Their messiness
- Their questions
- Their softness

They become *successful machines with souls on mute.*

🪞 3.7 COMING BACK TO THE SELF

But the exile doesn't have to be forever.

The return begins when:

- You name the wound
- You grieve the stolen childhood
- You reclaim the buried passions
- You allow yourself to disappoint those who benefit from your silence

"You are not selfish for choosing yourself. You are sacred for finally remembering your worth."

🛠 3.8 FROM EXILE TO EMERGENCE – HEALING STEPS

1. **Identity Reclamation Journaling**
   - "Who was I before the world told me who to be?"
2. **Voice Recovery Exercises**
   - Speaking desires aloud, even if trembling
3. **Authenticity Rituals**
   - Daily 5 minutes of "unproductive joy" (painting, writing, silence, dance)
4. **Therapy that heals narrative identity**
   - Especially narrative therapy, inner child work, and somatic practices
5. **Building a tribe of safety**
   - Finding friends, coaches, and mentors who love you *without* expectations

🎯 SECTION TAKEAWAY

You were never wrong for wanting more than performance.

You were never broken.

You were just **bending yourself to fit an illusion.**

Now?

You're allowed to *reclaim your wholeness.*

No more exile.

It's time to **come home.**

SECTION 4: HEALING THE FRACTURE

From the ruins of expectation to the rise of emotional truth

"You were never broken – only buried under someone else's idea of who you should be."

🌱 4.1 WHEN HEALING BEGINS

Healing doesn't begin in hospitals.

It begins in **honest rooms.**

Where a child finally says:

"I'm tired of being perfect."

Where a parent dares to ask:

"Did I push too hard?"

Where shame softens... and silence starts to speak.

Healing begins when the **cycle is named** – and someone chooses not to repeat it.

🔍 4.2 RECOGNIZING THE DAMAGE

Before healing, we must **see** the wound.

Not just the academic stress.

But the **emotional blueprint** created by years of performance pressure.

Patterns to recognize:

- Children who can't sit still – not from ADHD, but from **hypervigilance**
- Kids who can't celebrate success – because success feels like **another trap**
- Adults who avoid rest – because **rest triggers guilt**
- Individuals who shrink from praise – because **validation was always a setup for more expectations**

Once you name the pain – you stop passing it down.

4.3 RESTORING SAFETY IN PARENT-CHILD RELATIONSHIPS

Let's be honest.

Many parents don't mean to hurt.

They just don't know another way.

They love – but through the language of control, pressure, and fear.

"I did it for your good"

is not healing until it becomes:

"Did I ever make you feel unsafe to fail?"

What healing looks like:

- **Active listening:** Not fixing. Just hearing.
- **Permission to rest:** "You don't need to earn peace."
- **Celebrating effort, not outcome:** "I love how you tried."
- **Normalizing failure:** "What did this teach you?"
- **Open confession:** "I realize now... I was too hard on you."

Healing isn't about being perfect parents.

It's about being **present humans**.

4.4 THERAPY AS A TOOL FOR IDENTITY RECLAMATION

Therapy isn't just for those who are broken.

It's for those who are ready to break **the cycle**.

When children or adults enter therapy after years of performative upbringing, their healing often includes:

- Rebuilding self-worth **not tied to performance**
- Addressing **internalized pressure voices**

- Processing **conditional love wounds**
- Learning emotional regulation and identity rebuilding

🎙**Real-World Story:**

Riya, now 23, told her therapist:

"I don't even know what I like. All my life, I only did what would make my dad smile."

She began therapy after an anxiety-induced seizure before a college exam.

Today, she's pursuing **design,** not medicine.

She smiles now – not to please others, but because she **finally recognizes herself.**

That's not rebellion.

That's **healing through truth.**

4.5 WHEN PARENTS BEGIN TO HEAL

Let's not forget: **Parents are people too.**

Many were raised in fear themselves.

They didn't learn emotional safety – they learned achievement as currency for love.

"I didn't know another way"

is a beginning, not an excuse.

Healing for parents looks like:

- Reading books on emotional intelligence
- Going to therapy and confronting their own childhood wounds
- Apologizing to their children without defending their behaviour
- Rebuilding connection without demands

💬 **Example:**

Mr. Ghosh, 55, after his son dropped out of IIT:

"At first, I felt like I failed. But now I see... I just never asked what *he* wanted. Now we walk every Sunday. I don't ask about grades. I ask about his heart."

That's generational healing. In real time.

✍ 4.6 AFFIRMATIONS TO REWRITE THE SCRIPT

For **Children:**

- "I am more than my performance."
- "I am allowed to rest."
- "I can fail – and still be loved."
- "I am worthy of joy even when I am not perfect."

For **Parents:**

- "My child is not my project."
- "Their joy matters more than my pride."
- "I will not measure their worth with my fear."
- "I can be a safe space – not a scoreboard."

💎 4.7 CREATING A NEW FAMILY CULTURE

True healing is not just personal – it's **cultural.**

Imagine homes where:

- Dinner tables include "What made you smile today?"
- Report cards are reviewed with "How did this feel for you?"
- Failure is met with a hug, not silence
- Every child hears:

"You're already enough. Everything else is just a bonus."

This is not idealistic.

This is **possible.**

And necessary.

🔚 4.8 CLOSING THIS SECTION – FROM FRACTURE TO FLAME

You do not have to carry the pressure forever.

The pattern ends where **you** name it.

You are not broken.

You were bent toward someone else's dream.

Now, you get to rise toward **your own.**

This isn't about rejecting ambition.

It's about redefining success:

Not as gold medals and applause.

But as **inner peace, aligned purpose**, and **emotional freedom.**

🏆 The Trophy Wall

A Short Story Based on the Realities of Performance Trauma and Lost Childhoods

"Some children are raised to be winners. Others are raised to be warnings."

– From the diary of a child who never got to rest

💔 Prologue

The wall was beautiful.

Golden frames. Glossy shields. Crystal plaques.

It sparkled – even when the boy who earned it didn't.

Every visitor paused to stare.

"Wow," they said.

"What a brilliant child you have."

And every time they said it, Rihan's mother smiled.

And every time she smiled, Rihan's stomach twisted.

Because **he was never sure if they loved *him*** – or just the *wall*.

👦 Chapter 1: The Golden Son

Rihan was born into expectations.

Before he could say "mama," he was in phonics class.

By 3, he could write the alphabet backwards.

By 5, he was reciting multiplication tables at weddings.

His father, a former Olympiad finalist, said:

"My son will go further than I ever could."

His mother, a school topper turned homemaker, said:

"We will not repeat our mistakes through him. He will be *extraordinary*."

They didn't speak of feelings.

They spoke of **scores**.

They didn't praise effort.

They praised **results**.

And Rihan?

He stopped wondering if they loved him.

He started working to **earn it.**

🎯 Chapter 2: The First Miss

Age 10. State-level quiz finals.

He fumbled on one word: "Photosynthesis."

He got second place.

His father didn't talk to him for three days.

His mother cried – not for him, but for *what the neighbours would say.*

He wrote in his journal that night:

"When I win, they clap. When I lose, I disappear."

It wasn't the trophy he missed.

It was their *eyes.*

🩹 Chapter 3: The Cracks Begin

By 13, Rihan had panic attacks before exams.

He'd vomit in the washroom, wipe his mouth, and walk back like a soldier.

"No excuse," his father would say.

And Rihan believed him.

He stopped crying.

He stopped sleeping.

He stopped *being.*

The wall got fuller.

Rihan got **emptier.**

🧨 Chapter 4: The Breakdown

Age 16. IIT prep season.

The pressure was atomic.

Classes. Mock tests. Daily reviews. Sleepless nights.

One evening, he walked past the wall...

He stared at every medal...

And he *smashed* the biggest one.

It cut his hand. Blood dripped onto the marble floor.

His mother screamed.

His father slapped him.

No one asked, "Are you okay?"

That night, he wrote:

"The trophies can have me. I'm tired of being theirs."

🌧 Chapter 5: The Escape

Age 18. He got into IIT.

The family celebrated.

But Rihan... ran away.

He left a letter.

"You loved the idea of me – not me.

You wanted victory. You never asked if I wanted peace.

I'm not a trophy. I'm a person.

And I'm leaving – to find out who that person is."

🌱 Epilogue: The Real Wall

Years later, in a small hill town, a new wall stood.

No medals. No certificates.

Just messy art, Polaroids, scribbled poems.

Rihan teaches music now.

He runs workshops for children who were once "gifted and broken."

At the entrance of his studio, a sign reads:

"Here, your worth is not performance.

Here, we celebrate your presence."

A parent once asked, "Where are your accolades?"

He smiled and pointed to the kids laughing inside.

"They're not on the wall. They're *finally living*. That's my prize."

✨ Author's Note

This story is fiction.

But the pain behind it?

It's real.

It lives in schools, homes, counselling rooms – and often, behind perfect smiles.

Let us raise children for **who they are,**

not for **who we wanted to be.**

Because no trophy, no rank, no applause is worth the price of a lost childhood.

Let's teach children they're worthy – *before* they achieve.

Let's finally let them breathe.

Breaking the Cycle: Healing the Parent Within

Becoming the guardian your younger self needed – and your future self deserves.

"You are not the damage done to you. You are the architect of the healing you choose."

~ Anonymous

🌱 1. Re-Parenting Begins Where Criticism Ends

So many of us were **raised by broken mirrors.**

Parents who didn't mean harm – but had no language for love that wasn't performance-based.

Who only knew to motivate with guilt.

Who thought parenting was about shaping us into trophies – not sheltering us into safety.

And so we **became versions of ourselves they could clap for.**

Not the ones we truly were.

Healing this doesn't start by blaming them.

It starts by **meeting the wounded child within us** – the one who still flinches when they hear "Why can't you be more like...?"

💔 2. Generational Echoes: When the Child Becomes the Parent

Without healing, pain becomes inheritance.

We watch ourselves say things to our own kids that once broke us:

- "Is that all you could manage?"
- "You'll never succeed with that attitude."
- "Don't embarrass me."

We think we're correcting.

But often, we're **projecting** the same wound we swore we'd never pass on.

The child who wasn't heard becomes the parent who shouts.

The child who feared failure becomes the parent who never allows it.

Unless we pause – the cycle **never stops.**

🧠 3. What "Healing the Parent Within" Truly Means

To heal the parent within you means:

- To meet your inner child **with love** – not control
- To stop replicating your upbringing and **start reimagining** it
- To **validate yourself** without needing applause
- To say to your inner child:

"I'm so sorry you had to learn love through fear. That ends now."

It is **active parenting** of your inner self.

You become:

- The nurturer you missed
- The protector you needed
- The cheerleader you longed for
- The truth-teller your younger self prayed for

🧪 4. Case Study: *The Mirror Reversed*

Name: Rachit (32)

Profession: Startup CEO

Trigger: Couldn't accept his 5-year-old daughter's mistakes

Background: Rachit was raised by a military father – high discipline, no room for error. At 8, he was once locked out of the house for spilling tea. He never cried. He *froze.*

When his daughter spilled juice on the sofa, he exploded.

After she ran into her room sobbing, he told his therapist:

"I became my father. In the moment I wanted to protect her – I punished her. That night, I couldn't sleep."

Healing began not with affirmations, but with **apologies.**

He wrote a letter to his inner 8-year-old.

He hugged his daughter the next morning and said:

"I was wrong. You never have to be perfect to be loved."

Today, he keeps that juice-stained cushion as a **reminder of mercy.**

🩹 5. The 5 Practices to Heal the Parent Within

1. Witness Without Shame

Write down what hurt you as a child. Not to blame – but to **see clearly.**

"You're not too sensitive. You just needed to be seen."

2. Self-Forgiveness Rituals

You won't heal by being cruel to yourself for repeating what hurt you.

Say aloud:

"I forgive myself for parenting from pain. I choose presence now."

3. Model What You Missed

Were you never praised unless you won?

Start praising yourself – and others – for effort, not outcome.

"I'm proud of how I tried, even if I failed."

4. Embrace "Repair over Perfection"

Every parent gets it wrong.

Real love is in the **repair.** In the "I'm sorry. I'll do better."

5. Reparent Daily in Small Moments

- Eat when hungry – not when it's acceptable
- Rest without guilt
- Say "I need help" without shame
- Celebrate yourself – even when no one claps

You're not just healing your story.

You're **healing your lineage.**

🔁 6. Generational Healing: A Ripple Effect

"The moment you choose healing, you become the break in the bloodline – and the beginning of a new one."

When you parent from healing:

- Your children grow up without the shame you carried
- They feel safe expressing what you had to suppress
- They trust their bodies, minds, and emotions – because you modelled that safety

🍬 Long-Term Transformation:

- You stop parenting reactively
- You release control as a substitute for connection
- You replace fear with firmness, and guilt with grace

You become the sanctuary – not the storm.

🔥 7. Final Affirmation

"I am not the parent I was taught to be.

I am the parent I've chosen to become."

"And my child – whether born of body or soul – will know love without fear."

Part II: The Altruistic Facade: Outward Generosity, Social Validation, and Hidden Family Neglect

Chapter 1: Introduction

Parents and community elders are often admired for their selfless contributions–volunteering for charities, helping neighbours, leading church groups, or mentoring youth. These outwardly altruistic, nurturing, or caring behaviours win them praise and social approval. However, an unsettling paradox can lurk behind this benevolent public image. Many such individuals seem to crave the validation and admiration that come from these good deeds, even as they emotionally neglect their own families at home. In other words, the **"pillar of the community"** may privately be a cold, absent, or even cruel spouse or parent. The very person celebrated by neighbours for kindness might be experienced by their children and spouse as distant, unloving, or manipulative. For example, one recent case described a man regarded as a *"pillar of the community"* who was, behind closed doors, a tyrannical and abusive husband and father–his children noted *"it's like he puts on a mask"* when outside. While not all cases reach the level of overt abuse, the pattern of **duplicity** between public virtue and private neglect is a real and pervasive phenomenon.

This essay critically examines the dynamics of such behaviour, whereby parents and elders perform altruism for societal validation while failing to provide genuine emotional care within their own families. We explore the **psychological motivations** behind this outward altruism–grounding the discussion in concepts like social validation and the need for external approval. Social **validation theory** (broadly construed as the human need for social approval) will be used to understand why these individuals seek admiration through good works. We also consider the personality dynamics of *"communal narcissism,"* a form of narcissism characterized by a grandiose moral self-image and a craving to be seen as especially helpful or altruistic . Such individuals *"regard themselves as especially nurturing, understanding, and empathic"* and boast about their good deeds, yet ultimately their behaviour serves egoistic needs rather than true selflessness.

This part is structured in chapters to systematically address these issues. Following this introduction, **Chapter 2** will examine the phenomenon of pursuing social validation through altruistic behaviour, distinguishing genuine prosocial motivation from image-seeking behaviour. **Chapter 3** delves into the concept of communal narcissism and how outward "goodness" can mask narcissistic self-interest. **Chapter 4** applies family systems theory to understand how one member's need for external approval reverberates through the entire family unit. **Chapter 5** focuses on emotional neglect, defining what it entails and discussing its harmful effects on children's development and well-being. **Chapter 6** then centres on the perceptions and psychological impact on children who grow up in these families, while **Chapter 7** addresses the impact on spouses and marital relationships. **Chapter 8** broadens the view to societal and community implications: how society responds to these individuals and how public perception can either enable or eventually expose the duplicity. Finally, **Chapter 9** will provide a synthesis of theoretical insights and discuss potential avenues for addressing this issue, followed by a **Conclusion** in **Chapter 10.** Through a critical and scholarly lens, drawing on relevant theories and contemporary research, we aim to shed light on the hidden emotional neglect masked by an altruistic facade, and to understand the toll this duplicity takes on family dynamics.

In sum, while altruism and community service are typically laudable, it is crucial to recognize that **not all that glitters is gold**. Outward acts of care can be driven by a hunger for validation rather than genuine empathy. When parents prioritize the **approval of society over the needs of their own family**, the consequences can be emotionally devastating. By exploring this issue in depth, we can better validate the experiences of those children and spouses who *"find themselves in a particular bind because who would ever believe them?*, and we can challenge the notion that public benevolence always equates to private virtue.

Chapter 2: The Pursuit of Social Validation Through Altruism

One of the central features of the behaviour under examination is that the **outward altruism is performative**–it is driven less by pure compassion than by the desire to **seek validation, approval, or admiration** from others. Social psychologists have long noted that humans are motivated by a fundamental need for positive regard and social acceptance. **Social validation theory** (as used here) refers to the idea that individuals often engage in behaviours primarily to validate their self-worth through external approval and societal praise. In the context of outwardly caring parents or elders, their generous acts towards neighbours, friends, or the community at large become a means to an end: bolstering their own self-esteem and social image. This chapter explores the psychological mechanisms behind this pursuit of validation through "altruistic" behaviour.

2.1 Altruism Versus "Performative" Altruism

Altruism is traditionally defined as behaviour that benefits others at a cost to oneself, motivated by genuine concern for others' welfare. However, psychological research distinguishes between altruistic acts motivated by empathy or principle and those motivated by more self-centred goals. In the cases we are examining, the altruism can be considered *"performative."* The term **performative altruism** describes prosocial actions that are done **for show or personal gain**, such as enhancing one's reputation or satisfying an ego-driven need, rather than from authentic selflessness. As one expert on narcissism notes, *"performative altruism and humility, fashioned for gaining personal reinforcement, are also a form of grandiosity,"* even if these actions do tangibly help others. In other words, some individuals use good deeds as a stage performance–a *performance of virtue* that earns them applause, admiration, and a **"virtuous image"** that they find personally rewarding. They may be externally generous, but the **intent** behind the generosity is self-serving.

A classic psychological principle at play here is **impression management**, which is described by Erving Goffman's dramaturgical metaphor. Goffman observed that in social life people have a "front stage" where they perform roles for an audience, conforming to social expectations, and a "backstage" where they can drop the performance and be themselves. In the front stage of community life, the parent plays the role of the benevolent helper, carefully crafting an image that will earn social approval. They uphold all the norms of generosity and kindness in public, consistent with what society praises. But in the backstage of the home, away from the audience's eyes, their behaviour may starkly differ—neglecting the emotional needs of their spouse and children. This **dichotomy between front-stage and backstage behaviour** is precisely what causes confusion and pain for family members . The more these individuals invest in their *public persona* of the caring altruist, the more they may neglect or even suppress issues in their private family life, treating those as inconsequential so long as the audience sees a great performance. As Goffman's theory implies, such an extreme split between public and private selves can be inherently unstable and psychologically taxing, and it often leads to family members feeling they live with a stranger who is entirely different in private than the person known to the world.

It is important to clarify that seeking some degree of approval or appreciation is a normal human motivation. Prosocial behaviour often carries social rewards—people tend to like and esteem those who help others. The **difference lies in balance and authenticity**. In healthy cases, community-oriented parents balance commitments and derive satisfaction from both public service and private family bonds. Their altruism is not a mere performance but an outgrowth of genuine values, and they remain emotionally present for their family. In the cases we address, however, the **drive for validation is so dominant** that it eclipses genuine empathy and **reverses priorities:** maintaining the appearance of the "good person" becomes more important than being good to one's own family. The parent's identity becomes overly invested in *external* accolades at the expense of *internal* familial relationships. Psychologically, this reflects a form of **extrinsic motivation** (doing something for external rewards) rather than intrinsic motivation (doing it out of internal commitment to the value of caring). The actions—volunteering, caregiving, donating—are the same on the surface, but the underlying motivation shifts their meaning and consistency.

2.2 The Need for Approval and Contingent Self-Worth

Underpinning performative altruism is often a fragile self-esteem that depends on external validation. Researchers Crocker and Wolfe describe **contingent self-worth** as a condition where one's self-esteem is *"based on the approval of others or on social comparisons."* In such cases, successes and positive feedback cause spikes in self-esteem, whereas any lack of recognition or criticism causes sharp declines . Individuals with this contingent self-esteem become highly attuned to how others perceive them and are driven to engage in behaviours that will elicit praise. In our context, community caregiving offers a rich opportunity for visible good deeds that others will applaud—an alluring prospect for someone whose self-worth is contingent on external approval.

From a developmental perspective, such a deep need for validation often has roots in one's own upbringing. Many narcissistic or validation-seeking individuals were themselves raised with conditional approval—perhaps loved only when achieving or behaving in certain socially lauded ways. They internalized the notion that **love must be earned**, not given freely. As adults, they apply this to themselves by orchestrating scenarios where they can "earn" love repeatedly from an audience. The community becomes a surrogate for the *parental figure* that doles out approval. Unfortunately, this means they might not know how to simply accept or provide unconditional love in a private sphere. Instead, they continuously seek **reflected glory** from onlookers.

Neuroscientific and psychological studies of social reward show that receiving praise or recognition can activate the brain's reward centres similarly to tangible rewards. There is a kind of *"helper's high"*—a positive emotional boost from helping others—that is well-documented. But in healthy altruism, this positive feeling is a byproduct of compassionate action. In validation-seeking altruism, the *"high"* of praise becomes the primary goal. The person may become almost **addicted to praise**, needing regular hits of admiration to maintain their self-esteem. If a day or week goes by without external affirmation, they may feel restless or empty, because their self-worth reservoir quickly depletes without outside refuelling. This can partly explain why some such parents seem more **attentive to strangers' needs than their child's**. Helping a stranger might yield immediate gratitude and visible admiration, whereas tending to a child's emotional needs often provides no audience and no immediate acclaim. In blunt terms, **there's "nothing in it for them"** in comforting their own child—no one will see it or praise it. So their behaviour gravitates toward the arenas that *do* reward them externally.

Another concept relevant here is the **"social media" effect in modern validation-seeking.** With the rise of social networking platforms, people who crave validation have new avenues to display their good deeds. A parent might meticulously document their volunteering or the elaborate birthday parties they organize for other kids (or even for their own kids, but with an eye to posting about it) to garner online approval. The *"likes"* and comments serve as instant validation. This can further skew priorities: an evening might be spent arranging an Instagram-worthy charity event, while the parent scarcely speaks with their own child that day. As one analysis notes, *"platforms such as Instagram and Facebook serve as arenas for people to curate a public persona that elicits the approval of a broad audience... such behaviours often translate into neglect of family obligations, where a person's online presence takes priority over authentic family engagement"*. In extreme cases, family moments are only valued if they can be turned into social media content that bolsters the parent's image, rather than for the intrinsic joy or bonding they might bring. This is a contemporary twist on the age-old validation chase, amplifying it through technology.

2.3 Egoistic Motives Masked by Good Deeds

It is useful to consider how **self-enhancement motives** can masquerade as altruism. Psychologists talk about concepts like **"egoistic altruism"** or **"narcissistic altruism,"** where helping others satisfies one's own ego needs. One psychodynamic concept, introduced by early psychoanalysts and echoed by modern researchers like Sam Vaknin, is that some narcissists engage in **"narcissistic altruism"** to exert control or to feel superior by being the benefactor. They might foster dependence in those they help, thus gaining power or loyalty, or simply use charity to "keep score" of their goodness. In our scenario, a parent might constantly remind their family (and themselves) how much they do for others, implicitly suggesting their moral superiority.

This can manifest in a martyr-like stance: *"I sacrifice so much for everyone, and here my own family is ungrateful."* By painting themselves as an overworked saint, they deflect criticism for their inattention at home and instead induce guilt or silence in family members who might otherwise complain.

Social exchange theory provides another lens: in any interaction we often expect some form of reciprocation or payoff. While genuine altruism defies straightforward reciprocity, the payoff for the validation-seeking altruist is the **reputation** and **social capital** gained.

In essence, they are "paid back" not by the beneficiary but by society's admiration. Over time, that admiration can translate into concrete benefits too—better social connections, opportunities, perhaps even career advancement or honours. Such tangible rewards can reinforce the behaviour. But even in absence of tangible rewards, the **psychic reward** of being revered can be enough. This is why these individuals so eagerly volunteer for visible roles (head of the PTA, organizer of charity drives, public-facing committees) where their contributions will be noticed. They may be less inclined to do good deeds in quiet, unseen ways (e.g. listening empathetically to their child's concerns, which yields no public recognition).

It's instructive to consider the phenomenon of **moral licensing** in this context. *Moral licensing* is a cognitive bias where doing something good gives an individual a kind of "license" to not adhere as strictly to morals in other areas. In general, research finds that *"the moral licensing effect refers to a phenomenon where initial moral behaviour is used as an excuse for subsequent violations of social norms or misconduct"*. Applied to our scenario, a parent might unconsciously feel that because they have been so caring and generous to others outside, they have *earned a pass* to be neglectful or irritable at home. They might think (or act as if), *"I've spent all day helping those in need; I don't have to put effort into listening to my spouse's trivial problems"* or *"Since I'm such a good mother to the kids at school as a volunteer, it's okay if I'm less attentive to my own child's emotional upsets."* This rationalization process essentially permits them to **justify their neglect** of familial duties because, in their self-assessment, they have accumulated plenty of "moral credit" through their community service. Moral licensing thus maintains their positive self-image even as they fail in private roles—any guilt or doubt is assuaged by recalling their saintly actions elsewhere.

In fact, this dynamic often leads to a **double standard** in their behaviour: extreme patience and kindness for strangers or community members, but impatience or dismissiveness toward family. The parent might, for example, spend hours gently counselling a troubled teen in the neighbourhood, yet tell their own teenager to "stop whining" when that child expresses anxiety or sadness. To outside observers, the person seems immensely compassionate; to the spouse or child, the person seems oddly devoid of empathy at home. The stark contrast can be bewildering and hurtful for family members. It is as if the parent's **"compassion reservoir"** is used up on others, and nothing is left for home–or more accurately, the parent doesn't see investing compassion at home as necessary for their goals, whereas deploying it publicly is.

2.4 Social Norms and the Allure of Admiration

Society often reinforces performative altruism through its admiration of public service. Being known as a generous, community-oriented person brings **social status**. Sociologist Pierre Bourdieu might call it a form of *social capital*, and it can even be a form of **symbolic capital** where moral reputation increases one's influence and standing. In many cultures, there is strong normative pressure to appear like a "good parent" and a "good citizen." People who exemplify these traits are lauded. Thus, there is an external incentive structure: those who visibly take care of others often receive accolades, titles, awards, or simply social approval in conversation.

Our culture sometimes creates **personas** or archetypes such as "Supermom," "The Philanthropist," or "Community Pillar," which people may aspire to for the glory associated with them. A parent might relish being called "*the best parent on this planet*" or "*the most caring person in [their] social surrounding,*" echoing statements from the Communal Narcissism Inventory . These hyperbolic self-views–"*I greatly enrich others' lives,*" "*I will be famous for increasing people's well-being*"–illustrate how the communal narcissist's altruism is intertwined with grandiose expectations of recognition. They do not merely want to do good; they want to be **seen and remembered** as a doer of good deeds. This is a critical distinction. The focus on **visibility and legacy** ("I will be well known for the good deeds I have done") shows that the goal is not the deed itself but the personal reputation arising from it.

Furthermore, social validation operates in a feedback loop. When the community praises such an individual, it **reinforces the behaviour**. Family members may witness this cycle with frustration. For instance, imagine a mother who neglects her children's emotional needs, yet she is constantly praised by neighbours for being so helpful and kind to them. Every compliment or public thank-you she receives acts as positive reinforcement, encouraging her to continue prioritizing those outside interactions. It becomes harder for the children or spouse to assert their needs, because doing so feels like going against not just the parent but the whole community's perception of that parent. Indeed, some children in these situations lament that *"who would ever believe them"* if they complained, given their parent's glowing public image. The community, unwittingly, can become a sort of *enabler* of the neglect, by providing the narcissistic or validation-hungry parent exactly the praise and identity confirmation they seek, without seeing the private costs.

Social norms can also stigmatize those who voice dissent about such a beloved figure. A spouse who complains that "everyone thinks my wife is an angel but at home she ignores us" might be met with scepticism or told they are *overreacting* or *ungrateful*. This **social disbelief** silences family members and further empowers the facade. The outwardly altruistic parent likely is aware, at least intuitively, that their public deeds shield them from criticism. Some exploit this: they know that if they maintain the shiny public image, any private issues will likely be chalked up to the spouse or child being difficult or unappreciative. In this way, the pursuit of social validation through altruism doesn't just coincide with family neglect–it actively

undermines the family's ability to seek help or understanding. The social validation not only feeds the ego, but also provides a kind of *immunity cloak* against accountability at home.

In summary, the pursuit of social validation through ostensibly altruistic behaviour is a complex psychological strategy. It involves *performing goodness* to satisfy ego needs and contingent self-worth, thereby gaining praise, admiration, and a sense of identity as a "good person." This behaviour is encouraged by societal rewards and can be rationalized through mechanisms like moral licensing. However, as we shall examine in subsequent chapters, these ego-driven altruistic performances have a dark side: they often come at the direct expense of the individual's own family members, whose emotional needs are neglected or whose well-being is compromised. The next chapter will delve deeper into the personality profile often associated with this pattern—**communal narcissism**—to understand how an outward focus on being nurturing and altruistic can paradoxically coexist with a lack of genuine empathy and care in intimate family relationships.

Chapter 3: Communal Narcissism – Altruism as a Mask for Self-Enhancement

The pattern of outward altruism masking inner neglect finds a clear expression in the psychological concept of **communal narcissism.** Narcissism, in general, is characterized by an inflated self-image, a sense of entitlement, a need for admiration, and a lack of true empathy. While the classic narcissist (often called *agentic narcissist*) seeks status and admiration through achievements, power, or attractiveness (agentic domains), the **communal narcissist** seeks the same validation but through being seen as **especially prosocial and caring.** In other words, communal narcissists view themselves (and want to be viewed by others) as the most helpful, nurturing, and morally righteous people. This chapter examines how communal narcissism operates, and how it can lead to exactly the kind of discrepancy between public benevolence and private dysfunction that we are discussing.

3.1 Defining Communal Narcissism

Researchers Jochen Gebauer and colleagues formally introduced the term *communal narcissism* in a 2012 study, distinguishing it from the more familiar *agentic narcissism*. They proposed an **agency-communion model of narcissism**, wherein the narcissist's core self-aggrandizing motives (grandiosity, entitlement, need for esteem) can be expressed in different domains. Agentic narcissists claim superiority in agentic traits (e.g. intelligence, success), whereas communal narcissists claim superiority in communal traits (e.g. helpfulness, trustworthiness, generosity). In their studies, communal narcissists endorsed statements like *"I am the most helpful person I know"* and *"I am going to bring peace and justice to the world"* at very high rates. They genuinely hold an image of themselves as extraordinary benefactors and caretakers of others. However–and critically–despite **seeing themselves as highly communal**, others around them do not share this positive view. In fact, Gebauer et al. found a "low self-other agreement" for communal narcissists: these individuals rated themselves as very caring, but outside observers did not perceive them as particularly caring. This discrepancy hints at the performative or superficial nature of their "care." Outsiders, over time, may notice the lack of depth or consistency in the communal narcissist's altruism.

Communal narcissists are often socially skilled, at least initially. They know how to use the language of empathy and appear interested in others. They might publicly declare heartfelt commitments to good causes, recount their good deeds, and insist on their identity as a **giver, not a taker**. As one description puts it, *"They proudly announce how much they give to charity... They trap you in a corner at a party and whisper excitedly about how thoughtful they've been to their grieving neighbour. 'That's me–I'm a born listener!'"*. This portrayal by Craig

Malkin and Peg Streep illustrates that communal narcissists actively broadcast their compassion. They derive pride and a sense of uniqueness from believing (and having others believe) that they are exceptionally kind and nurturing. Notably, they often also harbour a disdainful attitude toward others whom they view as less charitable or "shallow" in comparison to their own lofty, meaningful pursuits. This reinforces their grandiose self-concept: others are petty or selfish, whereas *I* am devoted to higher causes.

The communal narcissist's **self-image** is thus one of moral superiority in the communal realm. But the same narcissistic dynamics of entitlement and lack of empathy lurk beneath. For example, communal narcissists may become **highly aggressive or defensive when their altruistic image is challenged**. If someone questions their motives or points out a failing (say, "You cancelled on your kids again to attend another charity meeting"), the communal narcissist is likely to react with anger, denial, or projection, rather than introspection. Their grandiose self-image cannot easily tolerate contradictions. In communal terms, this could mean they might accuse the accuser of being selfish or insensitive for even bringing up the issue, flipping the script to maintain their virtuous facade.

3.2 Pillars of the Community, Tyrants at Home

A hallmark of communal narcissism in the family context is exactly the outward-inward split we have been exploring. As one analysis succinctly states: "*Understanding communal narcissism explains why sometimes women and men who are largely viewed as 'pillars of the community' and known for their devotion to charities and other causes can be highly destructive and unloving in their personal roles as friends, husbands, wives, fathers, and mothers.*". That observation encapsulates the core paradox. These individuals invest heavily in the **community role** of the benefactor, gaining admiration and gratitude from friends, neighbours, congregants, or coworkers. Yet in their **intimate roles**—the roles that do not confer public accolades—they often fail to practice the empathy or caring they preach. They might even behave oppressively or manipulatively with those closest to them.

In communal narcissistic parents, this can manifest as a strict expectation that the family support the narcissist's altruistic image. The family is not nurtured for its own sake, but rather managed as part of the narcissist's overall appearance of a "good family." The communal narcissist may demand that the spouse and children participate in volunteer activities or always smile and behave in public to reflect well on the narcissist. One adult daughter of a communal narcissist mother recounted: "*My mother was the perfect hostess, a consummate housekeeper, sang in the church choir, and ran every fundraiser in our town... She was also cold and manipulative and unloving to me... By then, she'd become so territorial that the invites to chair this or that dropped away and even family members were finally able to hear my side of the story. But, of course, my mother never acknowledged her behaviour. She believed her own hype.*". Several key features stand out in this account. The mother epitomized the communal narcissist: publicly indefatigable in helping and organizing, yet privately "*cold and unloving.*" There was **drama and manipulation**–the daughter hints that the mother caused politicized conflicts in the organizations (a sign that the "giving" was more about power and ego than true collaboration). When the mother's aggressive pursuit of recognition eventually alienated others ("territorial" behaviour can occur when a communal narcissist vies for being the top do-gooder), she lost some public lustre, and only then were others willing to listen to the daughter's experiences. Tellingly, the mother **never admitted fault**; she "*believed her own hype*". This self-deception is common–communal narcissists often fully buy into the narrative of their saintliness, using it to rationalize or deny any harm they do in private.

From this example and others, we see how communal narcissists can put family members in a **bind**. The family knows the painful reality, but outsiders see the cherished persona. As long as the communal narcissist's public image is intact, *"who would ever believe"* the family's complaints?. The spouse or child who speaks up may be met with reactions like, *"How can you say that? Your mother/father is such a wonderful person!"* This disbelief can be deeply isolating for the family. It is a form of **secondary invalidation**: not only are their emotional needs neglected at home, but their perception of that neglect is disbelieved or invalidated by the community. This dynamic frequently leads to what some therapists call the *"gaslighting"* of the family by the narcissist and even by the community inadvertently. The narcissist will insist internally and externally that they are a great parent or spouse—after all, *"look at all I do"*. They might accuse the family of being too demanding or unappreciative, framing themselves as victims of an ungrateful family despite their saintly efforts for others. This rewriting of reality can cause children especially to **doubt their own feelings**, a topic we will explore more in Chapter 6.

It is noteworthy that communal narcissists often enjoy **initial admiration** in new groups, but this may not last. Gebauer et al. observed that communal narcissists, like agentic narcissists, can be well-liked at first due to their confident displays of virtue, but eventually, people catch on to the hypocrisy or insincerity. In fact, the fall from grace can be even more dramatic for communal narcissists once exposed, because people feel particularly betrayed by *false kindness*. As one paper noted, the communal narcissist falls out of Favor "even more drastically because of the hypocritical nature of his or her motives". Imagine a respected charity leader who is later revealed to have mistreated their family or perhaps embezzled funds; the public reaction is often intense anger because the moral facade has been shattered. This contrasts with a more openly selfish narcissist, whom people might have expected to be trouble from the start.

However, communal narcissists are often skilled at maintaining their facade for a long time, especially in environments that don't require close sustained contact. They might hop between social circles or volunteer projects, always finding fresh audiences who will take them at face value for a while. Meanwhile, their family suffers in silence, hoping others will eventually see the truth. It's a lonely experience to live with Jekyll and Hyde: a *Dr. Jekyll* adored by the town, and a *Mr. Hyde* who comes out at home.

3.3 Lack of Empathy and Emotional Invalidation

Despite their claimed empathy, communal narcissists fundamentally lack true emotional empathy. They may have cognitive empathy (the ability to understand what someone might be feeling or what is socially appropriate to express) which helps them perform caring behaviour convincingly. But genuine **empathic concern**–truly feeling and caring about others' emotions–tends to be deficient. In the family context, this lack of empathy becomes very apparent. The parent might be able to express sympathy and give comfort to a neighbour in distress (because it fits their role and perhaps because it's a short-term, performative interaction), but when their own child is upset, the parent shows impatience or indifference. The child's emotions do not offer the parent any ego reward; in fact, they might be seen as an annoyance or a threat if they contradict the parent's narrative of a happy family or a well-parented child.

Thus, communal narcissistic parents frequently engage in **emotional invalidation**: dismissing, minimizing, or mocking the feelings of their spouse and children. For example, a child saying "I'm sad you weren't at my recital" might be met with "Don't be so dramatic, I had more important things to do–you should be proud of what I was doing instead" or "Stop feeling sorry for yourself, I do a lot for you." Such responses both lack empathy and re-centre the conversation on the parent's needs and narrative. Over time, this teaches children that their emotions are not valued, and that the parent's self-image will always trump their needs. It can also train children to present a false front themselves, perhaps mirroring the parent's behaviour: they learn to hide their hurt and present an image of the grateful, content child in public.

In a spouse's case, a communal narcissist might respond to a plea for more affection or help at home with similar defensiveness. The spouse might say "I feel lonely, I wish we spent more time together as a family," and the narcissist might respond "After all I do for everyone, including you, you have the nerve to complain? Maybe you should try being less selfish." The clear message is that the narcissist's activities are beyond reproach (sacrosanct, even), and any emotional need that conflicts is an illegitimate complaint. This is classic narcissistic lack of empathy and turning the blame around. The spouse ends up feeling guilty or confused for having basic needs.

Communal narcissists can also use the **tools of altruism manipulatively**. They might give extravagant gifts or do ostensible Favors that were never asked for, then expect devotion or absolute loyalty in return. In a family, this could look like the parent who, say, pays for an expensive education or buys the child a car (a visible, public marker of being a "great parent"), but still never spends quality time listening to the child. Yet if the child ever voices discontent, the parent angrily points to the material gifts or sacrifices made: "*How can you say I don't care? I've given you everything!*" Such a parent confuses **providing for** or **treating** the child with emotionally **caring for** the child. The grand gestures often have strings attached–they are meant to reinforce the narrative of the parent's generosity. In public, the parent might ensure everyone knows about these sacrifices or gifts ("I've worked overtime to send my son to the best college"), reaping admiration. In private, the emotional neglect continues, but the parent feels absolved by these acts.

It should be noted that not every outwardly altruistic person who neglects their family meets the clinical criteria for narcissistic personality disorder. However, the **traits** of narcissism (especially communal narcissism) provide a useful framework for understanding the extreme cases. Many likely fall on a spectrum of narcissistic traits without a full disorder. Others might instead have traits related to **histrionic personality** (desiring attention), or simply be deeply insecure individuals using external achievements as a coping mechanism. In any case, the common thread is a person who prioritizes **self-enhancement via communal means** over authentic emotional bonds with family.

3.4 Self-Reflection and Denial

An important question is: *Do these parents and elders realize what they are doing?* The answer varies. Some communal narcissists are quite **conscious** of their hunger for recognition and fully embrace it—strategically managing impressions and aware that home matters bore them or feel like a burden. They might privately acknowledge, if only to themselves, that they find solace or excitement in public praise that they don't find in domestic life. However, narcissism often involves a thick layer of **denial and self-deception**. As the example said, the mother "believed her own hype". Many communal narcissists genuinely convince themselves that they *are* wonderful parents and spouses by virtue of being wonderful to others. They create rationalizations: for instance, "I'm working so hard for the community *for* my family's honour," or "My family should understand that my purpose in life is to help others—this is a higher calling." These justifications help them avoid confronting the inconsistency between their public kindness and private coldness.

Moreover, narcissistic individuals are notoriously resistant to feedback. Their defence mechanisms may include **projecting** their flaws onto others, **blaming** family members for any conflicts ("If the kids are unhappy, it's their own fault, I've given them everything"), or dismissing the spouse as "overly needy" or "jealous of my work." By externalizing blame, they maintain their self-concept as blameless.

The communal narcissist might also bask in the **subjective well-being** that narcissists often report. Interestingly, research has found that narcissists, including communal ones, often have high self-reported happiness or subjective well-being. They feel good about themselves (perhaps from all the admiration they solicit), whereas those around them suffer. As one article wryly noted, *"it's just the rest of us chickens who are unlucky enough to find one kind of narcissist or another in our lives who experience a distinct loss of [well-being]. Hardly seems fair, does it?"*. In a family, the narcissist parent might be quite content with life, clueless or indifferent to the distress of their spouse and children, who indeed experience reduced well-being.

In sum, **communal narcissism** provides a profile for many of the outwardly altruistic yet inwardly neglectful individuals. It explains how someone can reconcile in their mind the vast difference between their glowing public persona and their painful private relationships. They see themselves as *exceptional givers* and feel entitled to admiration for it, but they lack the true empathetic connection that would make them care about those closest to them. This personality framework helps us understand the individual's side of the story. In the next chapter, we turn to the family's side: how does the family adapt (or maladapt) to having a member who is consumed by seeking external validation? Using a family systems theory lens, we will examine the systemic effects on family roles, communication patterns, and stability when a parent or elder prioritizes societal approval over familial emotional responsibilities.

Chapter 4: Family Systems Theory – The Impact on Family Dynamics

Family systems theory posits that a family is an interconnected emotional unit, where each member's behaviours and roles influence the whole system's equilibrium. When one member—such as a parent—becomes intensely focused on external validation and community image, the entire family system must adjust to this reality, often in unhealthy ways. This chapter applies family systems concepts to understand the **duplicity** of outward altruism and inner neglect as not just an individual issue, but a family-level dynamic. We explore how boundaries, roles, and communication are affected, and how spouses and children respond (often dysfunctional) to the imbalance created by the validation-seeking parent. The goal is to show that the consequences of the parent's behaviour are **systemic**: the emotional neglect is not just a series of isolated incidents, but a pattern that **reshapes the family's functioning**, often leading to long-term dysfunction if unaddressed.

4.1 The Family as an Emotional Unit

In a healthy family system, parents provide both **instrumental support** (food, shelter, education) and **emotional support** (love, validation, guidance) to children, while spouses support each other. There are **boundaries** that protect the marital relationship and the parent-child relationships, and roles are flexible enough to adapt to stress while maintaining overall cohesion. The family ideally serves as a secure base (to use attachment theory terms) from which children can venture out and as a haven to return to for emotional nourishment.

When a parent diverts a large portion of their emotional energy and attention to *outsiders* (be it community members or public activities), the **family's internal emotional economy** suffers a deficit. Family systems theory would note how other members may try to compensate for this deficit. For instance, an older child might step into a caregiving role for younger siblings to fill the void left by the frequently absent or emotionally unavailable parent. This is a form of **parentification**, where a child is forced to act as a parent (to themselves, siblings, or even to the other parent). Alternatively, the spouse might over function in the domestic sphere–taking on all parenting duties, trying to be both mother and father figure (in a psychological sense) to the children–to keep the family stable. The spouse's life may become very insular, revolving around maintaining the household, while the other partner is outwardly focused. This can create a **split family experience**: one parent is the behind-the-scenes labourer, the other is the public representative of the family.

Boundaries in such families often become skewed. **Boundary** refers to who is involved in which subsystems and how information and emotion flow. A validation-seeking parent might blur the boundary between family and society by constantly bringing the outside world into the home domain—e.g., they prioritize outsiders' needs within the home, perhaps inviting guests constantly or imposing on family time to serve others. Conversely, they may block genuine family emotional content from crossing the boundary outward—projecting an image of perfection to the outside and forbidding family members from revealing any internal problems. This can instil a rule of **secrecy**: *"Don't talk about what happens at home, we must keep up appearances."* Dysfunctional families, especially narcissistic ones, often have such unspoken rules that "image is everything" and that the family must present a united, ideal front to the world. In our context, that could mean children are told never to complain or act unhappy in public, and spouses are expected to smile and praise the altruistic parent to others, regardless of how they feel privately.

One outcome is that the **family narrative**—the story the family tells about itself—becomes controlled by the narcissistic or validation-seeking parent. *Unspoken rule*: "We are a caring, happy family, and any evidence to the contrary will be ignored or punished." According to one psychologist, *"in a narcissistic family, the needs of the parents are the focus and the children are expected in various ways to meet those needs... there is also secrecy, neglect, unrealistic expectations, an impoverishment of empathy, and ongoing conflict."*. This description applies well here. The parent's need (for admiration) is primary; children must comply by playing their part in the show (unrealistic expectation of children to constantly praise or not need attention). There is neglect (emotional neglect of children's needs) and secrecy (hiding the neglect). Empathy in the family is impoverished because the parent doesn't model it or allow it authentically. Conflict might arise but is often suppressed or goes unresolved, leading to tension.

4.2 Roles: The Hero, the Scapegoat, and the Lost

Dysfunctional family systems often develop **role specializations** to cope with stress. In literature on alcoholic and narcissistic families, roles like the *"hero"*, *"scapegoat"*, *"mascot"*, and *"lost child"* are described. While originally noted in alcoholic family dynamics, similar roles can emerge in any family with a high level of dysfunction or one dominant dysfunctional member.

In a family with an outwardly altruistic but inwardly neglectful parent, one might see the emergence of a **family hero** child. Perhaps to gain the parent's approval (since warmth is scarce, achievement might be the only way to get attention), one child excels in academics, sports, or similarly public achievements. This child's success can also be co-opted by the parent as part of their image ("See, I'm such a great parent that my child is a star student"). The hero child, in striving for perfection, provides the parent with another source of pride and validation. However, this comes at a cost: the hero may feel immense pressure and may hide their own struggles to avoid puncturing the perfect family image.

Another child might take on the **scapegoat** role. The scapegoat is the one who, whether through rebellion or simply by being designated, carries the blame for family problems. If tensions rise or if the parent's behaviour causes issues, the parent can blame the scapegoated child: *"Your bad attitude is the reason we have tension here,"* or *"If you weren't so difficult, I'd be less stressed and more present."* The scapegoat's behaviour often responds to the dysfunction (for instance, a teenager acting out because they feel unloved), but the family narrative flips cause and effect, making the child's behaviour seem like the source of the trouble rather than a symptom. This absolves the parent of responsibility and reinforces their need to look good: they can say they *would* be an even greater community contributor or a more attentive parent *if only* this one troublesome family member didn't cause chaos. Outside the home, the parent might even subtly discredit the scapegoat child to others, ensuring that if the child complains about them, people will think the child is just acting out. This is tragically common in narcissistic family structures: *"When something bad happens...someone must be blamed for it. Typically there is a family scapegoat who is made to bear the main burden of the family's problems, frustration, and unhappiness, as well as the dominant narcissist's projected self-loathing."*. The scapegoat in our scenario might be the one who refuses to smile for the pictures or publicly challenges the parent's narrative, thereby becoming a threat that must be quelled or stigmatized within the family.

Another possible role is the **lost child**–a child who withdraws, becoming emotionally distant or invisible to avoid adding any burden. In the presence of a parent who is more interested in strangers than in them, a child may conclude that the best strategy is to not demand attention at all. They might retreat into solitary activities, show little emotion, and essentially disappear in the family system. This "lost" strategy is a way to cope with neglect: if overt bids for attention are fruitless or punished, the child stops making them. The lost child often suffers in silence, sometimes developing rich imaginary lives or secret hobbies. They can fly under the radar, neither contributing to nor disrupting the family image, thereby escaping negative attention but also receiving no positive attention. In adulthood, these individuals might struggle with expressing their needs or connecting with others, a direct outcome of their adaptation to an emotionally neglectful family.

The **spouse** of the narcissistic altruist also takes on roles. Often, they become the *enabler* or *appeaser*. Their life may revolve around supporting the narcissistic partner's activities (handling logistics at home while the other is away doing volunteer work, excusing the partner's absence to the kids with "Your dad/mom is doing such important work, we must understand"). They may play the role of the *cheerleader* in public, praising their spouse to others, even while quietly hurting. Some spouses find meaning in at least being part of the altruistic projects, effectively merging with the narcissist's cause to have some shared time or purpose with them. Others withdraw emotionally, leading parallel lives under the same roof—"emotionally divorced" within the marriage. In more toxic dynamics, the spouse might become another **target of blame**: the narcissistic parent might hold the spouse responsible for anything wrong at home (since they themselves are busy being perfect outside, any domestic issues must be due to the spouse's failings). Or the narcissist might triangulate, pitting the spouse and children against each other to deflect attention from the narcissist's shortcomings.

Family systems theory describes such triangulation and projection processes. Bowen's concept of the **family projection process** indicates that parents can project their emotional issues onto children. A parent who unconsciously knows they are failing the family might, for instance, project feelings of inadequacy by accusing a child of being ungrateful or flawed—externalizing the inner problem. The **emotional cutoff** is another Bowen concept, where family members, unable to resolve tensions, simply distance themselves. In our scenario, children upon reaching adulthood might cut off contact or greatly limit interaction with the parent to protect themselves, which ironically could mystify the parent who still believes they did everything right (after all, they were such a pillar of community, how could their own child estrange them?).

4.3 Strained Interactions and Communication

Communication in these families often becomes strained and inauthentic. Honest expression is curtailed by the dominating parent's need to maintain their narrative. This can lead to what family therapists call a **"pseudo-mutuality"** in extreme cases—a false appearance of harmony. The family might appear very close-knit and pleasant in public or at gatherings, echoing the altruistic parent's positivity. But behind closed doors, real issues are swept under the rug, and there may be a complete breakdown of intimate communication between the validation-seeking parent and other members.

Children learn that certain topics are "not safe" to bring up—especially anything that might be perceived as criticism or neediness toward the parent. They might not tell their parent about being bullied at school, for example, because the parent might dismiss it or compare it to "real problems" others face (thus again putting outsiders first). Instead, children suppress their hurts. Spouses may stop voicing discontent after repeated fights that go nowhere. Over time, a **wall of silence or superficiality** builds up. The family talks about schedules, chores, and perhaps the parent's projects, but not about feelings, doubts, or relational issues.

This inhibition of open communication further entrenches emotional neglect. A key insight of family systems theory is that problems can become **system-maintaining loops**. For example, the more the parent neglects the family for outside causes, the more the children act out or withdraw (depending on role), which then the parent uses as justification to focus elsewhere or blame, which then further hurts the children, and so on. Similarly, the more the spouse nags or pleads for attention, the more the narcissistic partner might frame them as the source of negativity, pushing away from them into outside admiration where they feel appreciated, which then of course makes the spouse more upset. These **feedback loops** can trap the family in a cycle that perpetuates the initial problem.

It's also important to consider extended family or close friends as part of the system. Grandparents or relatives might either buy into the facade (telling the children how lucky they are to have such an exemplary parent, thus reinforcing the parent and invalidating the kids), or they might sense something is off and try to intervene. If relatives **observe the negligence**, it can cause rifts. As noted in the user-provided case study content, sometimes relatives offering unsolicited advice or trying to intervene in the face of observed neglect can lead to more division. The validation-seeking parent may resent interference and see it as an attack on their character, escalating conflict. Case studies have shown "how the quest for external validation can fracture [the] family unit" and even extend conflict to the larger family circle. The more the parent is confronted, the more they may cling to their self-justification, potentially splitting the family into factions (those who support the parent's viewpoint and those who don't). The family system, which ideally provides unity, becomes polarized over the issue of the parent's behaviour.

Additionally, the **emotional climate** of the home in these situations is often characterized by tension, inconsistency, and a lack of warmth. Family systems often strive for homeostasis, meaning they resist change and try to keep things "normal" even if normal is dysfunctional. Thus, if a child or spouse tries to break the silence or challenge the status quo (for instance, a child having an emotional meltdown or a spouse insisting on therapy), the system might initially resist strongly. The parent might retaliate or the other family members might even side with the parent (having internalized the family's rules and image) to quash the disturbance. This homeostatic mechanism can keep the pattern locked in place for years.

Yet, this equilibrium is a false one because the underlying needs are unmet. Over time, **resentment builds**. The user's case study points out that *"the resulting discord can lead to disconnection, resentment and even separation between family members, promoting a hostile atmosphere that denies the fundamental purpose of family relationships."*. The fundamental purpose of family–to provide a nurturing, supportive environment–gets lost when external validation becomes the parent's focus. Instead of a source of support, family life turns into a source of stress and alienation for its members.

Family systems theory also emphasizes **intergenerational patterns.** We might ask: did the validation-seeking parent come from a family with similar dynamics? Possibly so. They might have had a parent who similarly cared more about image than emotional attunement (a common thread in narcissistic personality development). Thus, they are repeating a learned pattern. Likewise, without intervention, their children could internalize this model of relationships and carry it forward. A child might grow up and unconsciously choose a partner who also is emotionally unavailable, because that feels familiar, or they themselves might become a people-pleaser who neglects their own needs because that was normalized. In this way, the **cycle of emotional neglect** can propagate across generations, even if the outward form changes (maybe the next generation seeks validation at work or via social media, etc.). Bowen's concept of **multigenerational transmission** suggests that the level of emotional dysfunction can be passed down unless someone in the lineage achieves enough insight and differentiation to break the pattern.

4.4 Breaking the Family Illusion

For the family system to break out of the unhealthy pattern, typically a crisis or some form of external input is needed. Sometimes an event happens that "*pulls back the curtain*" on the parent's facade in front of others—perhaps a public incident of anger toward the spouse or a child's serious psychological issue coming to light. This can validate the family's experiences and force a reckoning. Family therapy or intervention can also help by providing a safe space to name and challenge the dysfunctional rules. However, getting a communal narcissist parent to family therapy is notoriously difficult unless they can be convinced it's in service of maintaining their image or some other face-saving rationale.

From a family systems view, **change requires adjusting the entire system**, not just the identified "problem" individual. Everyone must learn new ways of interacting. For instance, the spouse may need to stop enabling and start setting boundaries, even at risk of conflict. Children (especially adult children) may need to individuate and speak their truth, perhaps with support, and not play prescribed roles anymore. The narcissistic parent would need to confront how their behaviour impacts others and develop true empathy—this is challenging, but not impossible, especially if they can shift their source of self-esteem gradually from external to internal, or find healthier ways to feel significant that do not harm the family.

One suggestion from the user-provided content hints at a possible constructive approach: engaging the family collectively in meaningful projects. Instead of the parent seeking validation alone, involving the whole family in goals (like a family business or community project undertaken together) could theoretically unify them and redirect the source of validation to a shared accomplishment. The idea is that *"families can unify around shared goals... which not only provide a tangible means of recognition but also reinforces family bonds*. By doing good as a team, the external approval still comes, but it is attributed to the family as a unit, not just the individual, and thus might reduce the individual's ego dominance while *increasing* mutual respect inside the family. While this is an ideal scenario and may not always be feasible, it highlights that reorienting the validation source from *external individual* to *external collective* and finally to *internal familial* validation might be a path to healing. Essentially, the family learns to **validate each other internally**, so no one member must go seeking it outside at the expense of the others.

The family systems lens thus reveals that the outwardly altruistic, validation-seeking parent affects far more than their own image—their behaviour restructures the emotional landscape of the household. The system often contorts itself to accommodate the parent's psychological needs, typically to the detriment of open communication, healthy boundaries, and the emotional development of children. In the following chapters, we zero in on the experiences of the children and spouses themselves, which we have touched upon here. We will detail the psychological and emotional ramifications for them (Chapters 5 and 6), which are the human consequences of the systemic issues we have just analysed. Understanding the system lays the groundwork for understanding the **individual trauma and challenges** that children and spouses from these families often face.

Chapter 5: Emotional Neglect – The Silent Assault on Children's Well-Being

Despite the outward appearance of a "model family" that the altruistic parent tries to project, the children in such families often experience **emotional neglect** at home. Emotional neglect is the failure to attend to a child's emotional needs, such as love, support, validation, and responsiveness. It is an act of *omission*—what the parent does **not** do for the child, rather than outright abuse which is an act of commission . Emotional neglect can be subtle and invisible to outsiders, but its impact on a child's development and mental health is profound. In families where the parent is busy nurturing the world but not their own child, emotional neglect becomes the defining feature of the child's upbringing. This chapter defines emotional neglect, discusses why it often goes unnoticed, and details the short-term and long-term effects on children who grow up under such conditions.

5.1 What is Emotional Neglect?

Emotional neglect occurs when a parent or caregiver chronically fails to notice, respond to, or validate a child's feelings. This can take many forms: not offering comfort when the child is distressed, not showing interest or pride in the child's life, not providing affection or attention, or not creating an environment where the child feels safe expressing themselves. Importantly, emotional neglect is often not accompanied by physical neglect; materially, the child might have food, shelter, clothes, and even luxuries. It is entirely possible for emotionally neglected children to come from families that look very well-functioning from the outside—no poverty, no obvious abuse, perhaps even what appears to be involved parenting (if the parent attends events or provides things). This makes it a **silent assault** on a child's well-being: hard to spot, easy to deny, yet deeply harmful.

In our context, the altruistic, validation-seeking parent might superficially believe they are a "good parent" because they provide and maybe because they occasionally do some performative act of care for the child (like throwing a big birthday party, mostly to impress others). However, day-to-day, the parent may be psychologically **absent**. They might be preoccupied with their community work or phone calls from people they're helping. When the child comes to them with a problem or emotional need, the parent brushes it aside or says they don't have time. Feelings are often ignored or **discounted**. As psychologist Jonice Webb describes, *"growing up in an emotionally neglectful family, with your feelings ignored or discounted, has profound effects on how you feel as an adult, the choices you make, and your perceptions of yourself"* . The child learns that their emotions either don't matter or are burdensome. Over years, this can stifle the child's emotional development; they may become unsure of how to identify or regulate their feelings because no one validated those feelings in childhood.

One of the tricky aspects of emotional neglect is that it is often **unintentional**. Some emotionally neglectful parents do love their children and think they are doing the best they can—they may simply be blind to the emotional aspect of parenting, often because they themselves were raised with emotional neglect and know no different . In the case of the outwardly altruistic parent, they might even rationalize that their external good works indirectly benefit their child ("I'm making the world better for the next generation, including my child"). Or they see putting food on the table and providing opportunities as the extent of their duty, not realizing that emotional connection is a crucial part of raising a healthy child. Yet, regardless of intent, the *impact* of emotional neglect is damaging. It is widely recognized in mental health fields that emotional neglect is a prevalent form of maltreatment, often with **comparable or even more insidious effects** than some more visible forms of abuse . Because it leaves no physical scars, it can be harder to identify and address, leaving many children to suffer in silence.

In families with a communal narcissist or validation-seeker, emotional neglect might coexist with occasional **emotional abuse** (such as harsh criticism or shaming when the child's behaviour conflicts with the parent's desires). Emotional abuse and neglect are often grouped together as forms of psychological maltreatment, and they are among the most prevalent types of child maltreatment. A 2020 summary in the *British Journal of Psychiatry* emphasizes that *"emotional abuse and emotional neglect are among the most prevalent of childhood maltreatment types and [are] associated with a range of poor mental health outcomes."*. We will discuss those outcomes shortly, but the key point is that these experiences are common and harmful, yet often **under-acknowledged**. Society might not see an altruistic community leader as an "abusive" parent, but if they chronically ignore their child's emotional needs, that child is indeed experiencing neglect that can shape their psychological makeup adversely.

5.2 How Emotional Neglect Manifests for Children

Children in such families often internalize a few damaging beliefs and feelings:

- **Feeling Unimportant or Unworthy:** When a parent consistently prioritizes other people or activities over the child, the child concludes *"I must not be important"*. The child may feel *unworthy of love* or attention, reasoning that if even their own parent doesn't care, who will? They may not articulate this, but it shows in their low self-esteem. One common sentiment reported by those who had neglectful parents is a sense of emptiness or not being good enough. They might say, "I always felt like I wasn't as important as the church members my mom helped," or "I got the message that everyone else's needs came before mine." This can lead to the child later developing a tendency to **people-please** or overachieve, trying to earn love (repeating the dynamic set by the parent's behaviour).

- **Invisible or Overlooked:** A neglected child often feels invisible. Jonice Webb notes that when parents overlook a child's emotions, they *"overlook the deepest, most personal expression of who [the child is]. So sadly, they may not actually know [the child] in any kind of deep or meaningful way."*. This is painfully accurate; the child perceives that their parent doesn't truly *see* them. They might think, *"If I disappeared, would my parent even notice?"* In families where the parent is busy caring for others, a child might observe, "My parent knows all about the neighbour's kids' hobbies and dreams, but knows nothing about mine." This lack of feeling known is a profound form of loneliness a child can experience *within* their own family.
- **Guilt and Self-Blame:** Children often blame themselves for the lack of parental attention. It's too threatening to the psyche to think "something is wrong with my parent for not loving me," so instead the child thinks "something is wrong with *me* that makes my parent not love me properly." As Webb describes, many such children *"have spent their life feeling emotionally let down by [their] parents"* which makes it hard to feel love for them, yet *"you may have always blamed your lack of positive feelings on yourself and felt guilty about it"*. They

internalize the failure of the parent-child bond as their own failure. For instance, a child might think, "Maybe I'm too needy, that's why Dad doesn't spend time with me," or "If I were better (smarter, quieter, more helpful), Mom would love me more." This self-blame can become ingrained and lead to feelings of shame or beliefs that *"I don't deserve love/attention."*

- **Yearning and Anger:** The child often experiences a confusing mix of yearning for the parent's affection and anger at the parent's neglect. However, expressing anger toward the revered parent is usually forbidden (explicitly or implicitly). Thus, some children turn the anger inward (leading to depression or self-harm) or they misdirect it outward in rebellious behaviour or aggression toward others. They might be angry at the community for "stealing" their parent. Indeed, some children resent the very people their parent helps: they think, "Why do those people get my parent's kindness while I get nothing?" Such children might act out rudely when those people are around or sabotage events, trying unconsciously to get their parent's attention, even if negative. Unfortunately, this often backfires and leads to more scolding or labelling of the child as a problem (fulfilling a scapegoat role, as discussed).
- **Confusion and Cognitive Dissonance:** Especially if the community constantly praises the parent (*"Your dad is so great, he's helped us so much"*), the child experiences confusion: How can their parent be kind to others but not to them? Does the parent love them deep down or not? Is the parent a good person or not? This cognitive dissonance can impede the child's ability to trust their own perceptions. They see two different versions of the parent. In psychology of abusive dynamics, this is akin to *"intermittent reinforcement"* (though in this case the positive reinforcement is seen by others, not

necessarily felt by the child). The child might cling to hope: "Maybe one day Mom will be as kind to me as she is to others; it's my fault for not being like those others." Or conversely, the child might begin to see the parent as thoroughly hypocritical and lose respect, which brings guilt because society tells them they should love their parent. Living with such contradictions can stunt a child's emotional clarity and development of a coherent self.

- **Trust Issues:** A child who cannot rely on their primary caregiver to be there for them may develop an insecure attachment style. They may become **avoidantly attached** (learning to not seek support at all, since it's not forthcoming) or **anxiously attached** (constantly worried about abandonment and desperately seeking validation from others to fill the void). Moreover, because they witness kindness in public but meanness or indifference in private, they learn that people can wear masks. They might extrapolate that **no one's good intentions are genuine**, or that if someone is kind, it might hide selfish motives. This worldview can make it hard to form trusting relationships later in life.

5.3 Psychological and Emotional Consequences

The fallout of emotional neglect on children has been well-documented in psychological research. **Poor self-esteem, difficulty regulating emotions, higher risk of depression and anxiety**, and **difficulty in relationships** are common outcomes. One study notes that childhood emotional neglect predicts the development of depressive and anxiety disorders in later life. Another source highlights that emotional neglect is associated with maladaptive behaviours and adjustment difficulties in adolescence . Children of neglect often grow up feeling a sense of emptiness or a lack of fulfilment, sometimes described clinically as "*schemas*" of emotional deprivation. They may become highly independent and not ask for help even when they need it, or the opposite, constantly seek external validation and comfort in an exaggerated way because they are trying to fill an internal void.

Some hidden consequences include:

- **Alexithymia or Unawareness of Feelings:** Because no one responded to their feelings in childhood, these individuals might struggle to even know what they feel. They learned to numb out. As adults, they might say, "I often feel empty or numb rather than sad or angry, and I have trouble identifying my emotions." This is a coping mechanism from childhood–if feelings were ignored, better to suppress them entirely.
- **Depression:** Chronic feelings of loneliness and unimportance can fuel depression. Indeed, numerous studies connect childhood emotional neglect with later depression The person may carry an inner belief of being defective or unlovable, which is a core feature of depression.
- **Anxiety:** Growing up never knowing when you'll get attention or love, or constantly fearing you won't, can create generalized anxiety. There is also the anxiety of performance–some neglected kids try to be perfect to win their parent's affection, and that performance anxiety can generalize to other areas (school, work).
- **People-Pleasing or Difficulty Setting Boundaries:** An adult who as a child was neglected may become overly eager to please others (replaying the role of trying to earn love). They might also have trouble saying no, because they fear losing any scrap of affection or approval. Ironically, this can put them at risk of entering relationships where they are again taken for granted or even abused, perpetuating a cycle.

- **Anger and Aggression:** Alternatively, some who feel deeply hurt by neglect may have underlying anger that emerges in bursts. As children, they might have conduct problems, and as adults, they could become angry at partners or their own children without fully understanding why. Often, it's displaced anger from feeling unloved by their parent.
- **Lower Resilience to Stress:** Emotional support in childhood helps build resilience. Without that secure base, these individuals may find adult stresses harder to cope with. They didn't have the experience of someone comforting them in distress, so distress feels overwhelming and hopeless.

As one summary put it, *"children raised in such an environment can develop a deep sense of insufficiency if they cannot meet external expectations, leading to greater anxiety, depression and fragile self-esteem built only on the volatile nature of social approval."*. This line, drawn from the analysis of validation-seeking behaviour's impact, captures how the child might internalize the very value system of the parent. The child learns to measure their worth by external approval (since internal family approval was absent) and thus may chase achievements or other people's validation, much like the parent did, continuing the cycle. But because this is a "volatile" foundation, their self-esteem is fragile and prone to crashing when approval is not present.

Additionally, children in these families often **lack healthy role models** for relationships and self-care. They didn't see a parent model empathic listening or emotional regulation. They might not have learned basics of emotional literacy–how to name feelings, how to soothe oneself or seek appropriate support. If multiple children are in the family, the **sibling relationships** can also be affected. Earlier we mentioned how competition for the parent's limited attention can breed sibling rivalry. Indeed, when validation is scarce at home, siblings might vie against each other for what little crumbs of recognition exist. The user-provided content notes, *"family members* *can participate in competition for social recognition, thus eroding the support systems traditionally offered within family structures. Rivalry between siblings can exacerbate as children measure their success by social standards... undermining family ties".* Instead of siblings being allies, they may become competitors or turn against each other, further depriving each other of support. Some siblings might also resent one who seems to get more of the parent's limited attention (perhaps the "golden child" if one exists). This prevents them from uniting to cope; instead, each child feels more alone.

The **lack of secure attachment** with the primary caregiver can echo into all future attachments. Attachment theory tells us that an emotionally available caregiver is crucial for a child to develop a secure attachment style, characterized by feeling worthy of love and expecting others to be responsive. Emotional neglect typically leads to insecure attachment. An anxiously attached child might become clingy in other relationships, constantly fearful of neglect or abandonment (replaying their early experience). An avoidantly attached child might act like they don't need anyone, staying distant even with friends or later romantic partners, because closeness is associated with disappointment. Both patterns can hinder healthy relationship formation in adulthood, potentially leading to further loneliness or cycles of conflict and dissatisfaction.

Perhaps one of the saddest outcomes for children of these families is that they **miss the simple joy of childhood feeling loved and valued for who they are.** They often describe their childhood in retrospect as having something big missing, even if they can't put a finger on it. They might have had birthday parties, plenty of toys, and maybe impressive experiences arranged by the parent (especially if the parent wanted to show off), but they lack warm memories of cuddles, heartfelt talks, being comforted when sad, or being celebrated in private, intimate ways. This void can be experienced in adulthood as a kind of nostalgia for a childhood they never had–a sense of grief or envy when they see others talk about supportive parents.

As adults, some will seek therapy and come to name their experience as childhood emotional neglect (CEN). That recognition itself can be powerful, as they realize it wasn't their fault—they had *"a well that was dry"* when they repeatedly went to it seeking emotional sustenance. Coming to terms with the idea that *"It's not that I was unlovable; it's that my parent was unable or unwilling to love me in the way I needed"* can be a painful but freeing realization. It allows for healing to begin, but it often takes significant work to rebuild one's sense of self and learn the emotional skills one missed.

In closing this chapter, it's crucial to highlight that **emotional neglect is a form of trauma**. It may not be trauma in the sense of a single life-threatening event, but it's a chronic developmental trauma, an ongoing absence of something essential. It shapes the brain and psyche. As one mental health writer put it, *"Emotional neglect is considered a form of trauma, as it can have long-lasting and profound effects on a person's emotional and psychological well-being "* . Children need emotional attunement the way plants need water; without it, they wilt in various ways. In families where a parent's altruistic energies are directed outward and little is left for the children, the children are effectively left in an emotional desert. The next chapter will continue by examining the impact on the other often-neglected victim: the spouse or partner of the validation-seeking parent. While children suffer in unique ways due to their dependence and development, spouses experience their own form of emotional neglect and psychological strain, which we will now explore.

Chapter 6: The Spouse's Struggle – Marriage to a Socially-Adored but Emotionally Distant Partner

Behind many outwardly admired do-gooders stands a spouse or partner who intimately knows a different person than the public sees. Being married to or in a partnership with someone who seeks validation in the community while neglecting their home responsibilities can be an isolating and demoralizing experience. The spouse often bears the brunt of practical duties, suffers lack of emotional support, and may even endure direct emotional abuse or manipulation. This chapter focuses on the **spouse's perspective**: how these relationships function (or malfunction), the emotional toll on the partner, and the dynamics of marital interaction when one partner is consumed by the pursuit of external admiration. We will also consider how societal perceptions can compound the spouse's difficulties, like how they affect the children.

6.1 The Emotionally Abandoned Partner

Spouses of individuals who are generous to everyone except at home often report feeling **emotionally abandoned**. They might describe their marriage as lonely, saying things like, "I feel like a single parent," or "My partner is married to their work/causes, not to me." The neglect they experience is somewhat different from what children experience because a spouse is (in theory) a peer adult who can articulate their needs and has some agency to leave or demand change. However, many factors keep spouses in such relationships for extended periods: love (or memories of love from earlier in the relationship), children (not wanting to break the family), financial dependence, cultural or religious beliefs about marriage commitment, or simply the hope that the partner will change or "come home" emotionally one day.

The daily reality for the spouse can involve a heavy **imbalance in labour and affection**. For example, one spouse might handle all the household chores, childcare, and logistics while the other is constantly out organizing charity events or working late "for the greater good." While supporting a partner's noble endeavours can be tolerable when there is reciprocal care, in these cases the imbalance is extreme and without proper appreciation. The altruistic partner may take the spouse's contributions for granted, as if it is simply their role to free the altruist to do their important work. There may be little gratitude expressed privately, even if the altruist publicly thanks their spouse performatively at times (more for image than sincere appreciation).

Emotionally, the spouse likely receives minimal intimacy. Conversations might revolve around the busy partner's activities, or logistics, with scant time spent on the spouse's feelings, challenges, or the couple's relationship. Attempts by the spouse to seek closeness may be met with disinterest or annoyance. For instance, trying to plan a romantic weekend might be impossible because the partner's schedule is full of community commitments. When emotional issues are brought up, the partner may dismiss them: *"I'm too tired for this,"* or *"Can't you see I have more important things on my mind?"*. Such responses are invalidating and send the message that the spouse's emotional needs are trivial. Over time, the partner learns not to ask, not to expect, and they emotionally withdraw to protect themselves from repeated rejection.

Research on marriages with narcissistic individuals shows that **relationship satisfaction tends to be low** and psychological distress high for the non-narcissistic partner . Narcissistic partners (which communal validation-seekers often are) "struggle with providing genuine emotional support and empathy" and "often prioritize their own needs, desires, and emotions over those of their spouse". This aligns perfectly with what the spouse in our scenario endures. The spouse might frequently feel *"exhausted and drained"* because they are giving out emotionally (and often physically, managing home duties) without getting nurtured in return. Indeed, a description from a counselling perspective notes: *"Narcissistic partners often prioritize their own needs and desires over their partner's emotional well-being. They may show a lack of empathy and fail to provide emotional support... leaving the other person feeling neglected and unimportant."*. This quote encapsulates the spouse's predicament: neglected and made to feel unimportant. It is not uncommon for such spouses to question their sanity or their worth: *"Am I asking too much? Maybe I am selfish for wanting more from* *them when they're doing so much good outside."* The narcissistic partner might even reinforce this by telling them they are selfish or unsupportive if they complain, thus gaslighting them into doubting the legitimacy of their needs.

6.2 The Public Facade and Private Reality in the Marriage

One of the most painful aspects for spouses can be the **public-private split.** Similar to children not being believed, spouses also encounter the disbelief or minimizing by others. Friends might say, "You're so lucky to have a husband who is such a great guy," or "Your wife is an angel, I'm sure she's equally wonderful at home!" The spouse may smile and say nothing, but inside they might be seething or aching. If they confide in friends or family about their unhappiness, they might get responses like, "Well, at least he's not cheating or beating you; he's doing good things," or "Try to be more supportive; she has a lot on her plate helping others." These responses show a lack of understanding that **emotional neglect is real harm**. Just because the cause of the neglect is the partner's socially praised activities, it doesn't cancel out the pain of the neglected spouse. Unfortunately, the community that admires the altruistic partner can inadvertently invalidate the spouse's experiences, much like they do for the children.

Some spouses internalize the communal image so much that they also maintain the facade, sometimes out of pride or not wanting to appear like their marriage is less than ideal. They may attend events with their partner, smiling and playing the role of the supportive husband or wife. They might post on social media praising their partner's accomplishments (perhaps hoping to win a morsel of their partner's affection by boosting their ego). This *"front stage"* collusion means the spouse partakes in the performance that all is well, even as privately they feel empty. It's not unlike those in high-profile marriages or ministry families who keep problems secret to avoid scandal or judgment.

Other spouses, however, may eventually reach a breaking point. Resentment can build as years go by. They might attempt to fight or demand the partner change. These fights can turn ugly, particularly if the validation-seeking partner employs gaslighting or blame-shifting. A communal narcissist might respond to a spouse's pleas for more time together with something like, "You're just jealous of the attention I get" or "You're trying to hold me back from doing good; you should be ashamed of yourself." In some cases, the conflict can escalate to emotional abuse or even physical intimidation. The Irish Times case mentioned earlier is an extreme yet illustrative scenario: a wife described her husband as a "*tyrant*" at home, shoving her and frightening the children, even though he was a beloved community figure. She said, *"It's like he puts on a mask when outside the house,"* confirming how stark the contrast was. Not all cases involve physical aggression, but many involve **emotional abuse**, such as yelling, controlling behaviours, and intimidation behind closed doors. The spouse, in these cases, lives in fear and confusion: how can the person who speaks so gently to a stranger turn and speak with rage to me?

The **power dynamics** in such marriages often favour the altruistic partner, especially if they have the community's admiration. The spouse may feel they have little leverage to insist on change. The altruistic partner might even leverage their status to isolate the spouse. For example, if the spouse complains to a counsellor or religious leader and that leader is also enamoured with the altruist, they might side with the altruist or downplay the spouse's perspective. This can further trap the spouse, making them feel they have nowhere to turn where they will be believed over the charismatic, "saintly" partner.

6.3 Emotional and Psychological Toll on the Spouse

Spouses enduring chronic emotional neglect and possible abuse from a validation-seeking partner can suffer a range of psychological harms:

- **Depression:** Feeling unloved and stuck in a one-sided marriage can lead to depressive symptoms. The spouse may feel hopeless that things will ever change, and a kind of learned helplessness can set in, especially if prior attempts to improve the relationship were thwarted. They might start doubting their own worth, thinking "Maybe I am boring or not good enough; that's why my partner prefers spending time elsewhere."
- **Anxiety and Hypervigilance:** Living with a partner who might blow up if challenged, or whose mood is unpredictable (kind to others, irritable at home) can make a spouse anxious. They might walk on eggshells to avoid conflict, similar to abuse victims in other contexts. They can develop a constant state of alertness, worrying when the next emotional outburst or passive-aggressive barb will come.
- **Low Self-Esteem:** Narcissistic partners often erode their spouse's self-esteem over time. They might compare the spouse unfavourably to others ("Look at so-and-so's wife, she supports him without complaint; why can't you be like her?" or "Other husbands understand the importance of my work better than you do"). These comments, plus the implicit message that "you're not interesting or worthy enough for my attention," can make the spouse feel inadequate and unlovable.
- **Social Withdrawal:** The spouse may withdraw from social circles out of embarrassment or fatigue. It's draining to keep up appearances, and they might avoid gatherings to not face the façade or to keep from saying something that contradicts the script. Also, if the community is charmed by the partner, the spouse might feel they have no allies who truly see their side. This isolation can deepen their dependence on the very

partner who is neglecting them, because they feel they've lost other support networks.

- **Physical Health Problems:** Chronic stress in a marriage can manifest physically. Spouses may experience headaches, fatigue, insomnia, or stress-related illnesses. Some might develop anxiety-related conditions like gastrointestinal issues or high blood pressure. In a way, the body can express what the person is suppressing – the stress finds an outlet.
- **Loss of Identity:** Many spouses find that they have subsumed their identity either into the role of caretaker (for kids and home) or as an appendage to their famous altruist partner. They might say, "I feel like I lost myself in this marriage." Their own passions or career might have been put on the back burner to accommodate the partner's life. As a result, they might reach midlife feeling a sense of emptiness or not knowing who they are anymore outside the marriage.

Some spouses eventually choose to separate or divorce if conditions allow. Leaving a communal narcissist can be difficult, however. Such individuals may try to preserve their image by **manipulating divorce proceedings** or turning the community against the spouse, painting them as the villain. For example, a narcissistic partner might claim the spouse abandoned them because the spouse is selfish or unstable, rather than acknowledging their own role. This can lead to nasty custody battles or social fallout where the spouse is ostracized by people who only see the altruistic person's side of the story. Despite these obstacles, many spouses do find the courage to leave when the pain outweighs the fear, especially once children are grown or if they secure external support.

For those who stay, some reach a level of **detached acceptance** – a kind of emotional divorce where they no longer expect partnership and instead focus on other fulfilling areas of life (children, friends, personal hobbies) to get their emotional needs met. They might make peace with the arrangement if direct confrontation never yields change, essentially living parallel lives under the same roof. While this might quell constant conflict, it's more a survival strategy than a truly healthy marriage. It can allow the family to function on a superficial level but leaves the spouse's deeper needs unresolved.

6.4 When the Spouse Awakens

There are times when a spouse "awakens" to just how unhealthy the situation is. This could be triggered by an external event: maybe a friend going through something similar, or reading about narcissistic abuse which suddenly casts their experiences in a new light, or a counsellor validating that *yes, you are being neglected/abused.* Sometimes, if the children begin to suffer obvious issues (like a child's depression or misbehaviour draws attention), the spouse realizes they must act to protect the children and themselves. This awakening can lead to empowerment: the spouse might start asserting themselves, seeking therapy (with or without their partner), or setting firmer boundaries.

For instance, they may tell the partner that they will no longer lie to cover for them. Or they might insist the partner attend marriage counselling if they want to save the marriage. The reaction of the validation-seeking partner can vary: some might flat-out refuse and further villainize the spouse for making demands. Others, if they fear losing the marriage might comply superficially – though therapy with narcissistic individuals often fails unless the person truly acknowledges their issues. In some cases, a shock like the spouse truly walking out might jolt the altruistic partner into some self-reflection (especially if their image is at risk due to a public divorce). But genuine change is rare without deep personal work by the neglectful partner.

From the spouse's perspective, gaining support and validation from outside the immediate community is vital. This could be a support group (even online forums for partners of narcissists), a therapist, or a trusted friend/family member who understands. Knowing that they are not "crazy" or "overreacting," and that others have experienced similar duplicity in partners, helps them rebuild their self-trust. With support, they can decide whether to attempt to repair the relationship (if possible) or to plan an exit strategy if it appears unfixable.

Spouses must also work on **self-care and re-finding themselves**. Over the years, they likely neglected their own needs as much as they were neglected by the partner. Part of healing is re-engaging in hobbies, career, or social life independently of the partner's shadow. This can improve their well-being regardless of the marriage outcome. Some spouses even discover that they had been enabling or reinforcing the partner's behaviour in small ways, and by changing their own responses (not covering up, not always putting the partner's needs first, frankly calling out the hypocrisy in private without fear) they can regain a sense of agency and dignity.

In some narrative accounts, when the validation-seeking parent eventually ages or loses some of their public lustre, the spouse faces a new challenge: the partner might suddenly demand the family's attention (when outside admiration wanes) or become depressed themselves. The spouse might feel it's "too little, too late" or they may compassionate but burned out. It's a complex dynamic if tables turn. However, many communal narcissists maintain their denial and self-absorption lifelong, so some spouses remain estranged emotionally even if physically together until the end.

To sum up, spouses in these marriages endure a relationship that is **imbalanced, unsupported, and often unhealthy**. They often feel like they share their partner with the world, and the world always gets the best part while they get the leftovers or worse. The psychological toll is akin to that experienced by spouses of workaholics or addicts, but with the twist that society praises the very thing that is destroying the marriage (the partner's "good" work). This can make it harder to seek help or even to label the problem. Recognizing that *neglect is neglect*, and that a vow of marriage implies emotional presence, not just physical provision or social status, is key. The spouse's journey is one of validating their own reality, coping with or escaping the toxicity, and healing their self-worth.

Having examined both the children's and spouse's experiences, we see a pattern: the internal family system suffers greatly while the external social system applauds. This dichotomy between outer admiration and inner misery is a central theme. In the next chapter, we will explore more about the role of society and community in either perpetuating or potentially addressing this duplicity. We will consider how cultural expectations, stigma, and collective blindness to emotional neglect can allow these situations to persist, and what shifts might be needed to better support families behind the facade.

Chapter 7: Societal Perceptions and the Reinforcement of Duplicity

The issue of parents and elders who play the saint in public but neglect their families is not only a private matter–it's interwoven with societal attitudes and perceptions. Society often plays a role in **enabling** these patterns, at least initially, by showering praise on the outward behaviours without awareness of the private reality. This chapter analyses how community and cultural factors reinforce the duplicity, and how public perception can shift once the truth emerges (if it does). We also discuss the challenges in addressing such situations openly due to the social capital and sometimes **celebrity-like status** these individuals accrue. Ultimately, we consider the need for greater societal awareness of emotional neglect and a more balanced view of altruism that includes accountability for one's family responsibilities.

7.1 The Halo Effect and Social Applause

One key social-psychological concept at work is the **halo effect.** This is the tendency to assume that because a person excels or is virtuous in one domain, they must be virtuous in others. If someone is known to be extremely charitable or caring in the community, people infer that they must also be a good spouse, a loving parent, a morally upright person all around. This halo effect makes people less likely to suspect or believe any allegations of home neglect or abuse by that person. It casts a kind of **glow** around them that can blind others to evidence that doesn't fit the glowing image.

As a result, community members may unconsciously dismiss signs of a problem. For example, if a child of the person is acting out or seems troubled, outsiders might not connect it to parenting issues—they might blame peer influences or the child's own temperament, because they can't imagine the "wonderful parent" is part of the problem. Likewise, if the spouse seems unhappy or withdrawn at social gatherings, people might chalk it up to the spouse's personal issues, certainly not the fault of their esteemed partner. This reflects a kind of **societal denial or complicity**, not out of malice but out of the difficulty of reconciling the idea that a person who is a community hero might be a family zero (or worse).

Moreover, society tends to **valorise visible acts of service**. High-profile charity or community work often gets recognition—awards, public thank-you, media coverage. People who volunteer or lead in community initiatives gain social currency. In some cultures or communities, being heavily involved in church, school, or civic groups is also tied to one's social identity and respectability. There can even be competition among families to be seen as the most giving or community-minded. In such an environment, a person who pours themselves into community service might be seen as a role model, and their family held up as an example of the "right values". This can add **social pressure on the family** to conform to the image. The spouse and children might feel compelled to keep any problems hidden to avoid tarnishing the family name or facing backlash for "ruining" the community's high opinion of the altruist. Essentially, the community's adulation can inadvertently **silence the victims** by making them feel they would be betraying not just the individual, but the collective good, if they spoke out.

Society also often subscribes to the belief that parental goodness is evidenced by how much they sacrifice for their children or for others. Some of these parents ironically get community praise as "great parents" because of things like, say, organizing youth events or advocating for children's causes. Outsiders might say, "He cares about kids so much, he's always coaching and mentoring–what a great dad!" without realizing he hardly speaks to his own kids. This dissonance is not apparent to them because they see the effort the parent puts into children, just not *his* children. Similarly, a mother who runs fundraisers for the school may be assumed to be very involved in her children's education, even if at home she doesn't help with homework or know her child's friends.

The **virtue signalling** aspect of communal narcissism aligns well with modern social media. These individuals may post frequently about their good deeds or the causes they support, curating an online identity as a benevolent caregiver. Social media provides constant opportunities for short bursts of validation (likes, shares, positive comments). The community, in a broader sense including one's online network, reinforces the person's ego each time they approve of these posts. Meanwhile, the family's less photogenic reality is rarely if ever shared online. This creates a public archive of apparent virtue that further entrenches the person's reputation.

7.2 The Dilemma of Intervention

Because the socially-admired person often holds some level of status or authority, it can be tricky for external systems to intervene even if concerns arise. Teachers, for example, might notice that a child is emotionally struggling. But if that child's parent is the PTA president known for being so caring, the teacher might hesitate: "Could it really be issues at home? The parent seems so involved and kind." If they do bring up concerns, the parent might use their community standing to deflect, possibly saying the child is just spoiled or has problems, implicitly suggesting the teacher is mistaken.

In cases of outright abuse, sometimes community standing has shielded perpetrators for a long time (for instance, cases of clergy abuse often involve beloved figures who no one wants to believe did wrong). In emotional neglect, which is harder to pin down legally or visibly, the threshold to trigger outside concern is higher. Unless the children's mental health deteriorates to a crisis point (like a suicide attempt or running away) or there's clear evidence of abuse, neighbours or authorities rarely step in for "just" emotional neglect—especially if the parent is outwardly respectable. This is why some experts call emotional neglect an "invisible" form of harm.

Society also has cultural scripts that can excuse the neglectful behaviour. For instance, the narrative of the **"provider who works long hours for the family's sake"** can mask what is workaholism or avoidance of family. A parent might not be helping at home, but society says "well, he is working so hard so his family can have a good life." The parent might not actually need to work that much or might be choosing to do extraneous things for personal fulfilment, but culturally we often excuse especially fathers in this way. In our altruism scenario, the analogy is "They are doing God's work/important community service, so the family should understand and support that." This can be a noble truth in moderation, but as we see, it can become a rationalization for chronic neglect.

The spouse's complaints might also be minimized by well-meaning friends with phrases like, *"You have to share your husband with the world, he's a good man,"* or *"Your wife has a big heart, try not to be too demanding."* These remarks show how the **collective expectation** is that the spouse (and family) should essentially sacrifice their own needs because the parent is doing something praiseworthy. The spouse is pressured to fall in line as a behind-the-scenes support player. If they rebel against that role, they risk social scorn. This dynamic can be particularly strong in communities that preach selflessness as an absolute virtue; the spouse might even question themselves, "Am I being selfish to want more of my partner's time? Everyone else seems to think so."

7.3 When the Facade Cracks

Sometimes, over the years, the truth begins to seep out. It could be through the testimony of grown children, a public marital conflict, or inconsistent behaviour that more people witness. As one analysis we cited noted, *"the communal narcissist enjoys initial admiration but will fall out of favour even more drastically because of the hypocritical nature of his or her motives"*. Hypocrisy, once revealed, can swiftly reverse public opinion. Those who were ardent admirers can become some of the harshest critics, feeling deceived or foolish for having believed the facade.

Examples of this in real life include cases where respected public figures (like a philanthropist or activist) are later revealed to have abused their family. The media and public often express shock– "How could someone who did so much good do something so bad?" But once evidence is clear, the narrative switches to condemning that person as a fraud. If the person is a prominent community figure, there might be public fallout: loss of positions, withdrawn honours, etc. In a smaller community context, the person might find themselves socially ostracized if enough people believe the spouse's or children's accounts. The earlier Psychology Today piece described how, with communal narcissists, once people *"catch on,"* admiration can turn to dislike swiftly, and they *"fall out of favour"*.

However, the transition isn't always smooth or unanimous. There are often **camps of believers and sceptics**. Some supporters may cling to the idea that the person is still fundamentally good and that perhaps the family is exaggerating. Especially if the person is deeply enmeshed in a church or tight-knit group, there can be defensive reactions.

They might use rhetoric such as, "*Let he who is without sin cast the first stone,*" effectively urging people to overlook the transgressions because of the person's good works. In other cases, cognitive dissonance may cause them to minimize the severity: "*Sure, he wasn't perfect at home, but everyone has flaws–think of all the people he helped, it outweighs that.*" This is a controversial moral calculus, but it does happen.

From a societal perspective, these situations raise the question of what we value and how we define a "good person." If someone is altruistic to strangers but cruel to their own family, how should they be judged? Different people answer differently. Some argue that charity should begin at home and failing one's primary obligations invalidates one's external good deeds to an extent. Others compartmentalize the two. Ethically, it's a complex debate. But practically, when the facade cracks, communities often feel a sense of betrayal. This can lead to broader scepticism–people may become less trusting of public altruism, wondering if others, too, have secrets. Unfortunately, that can cast unfair suspicion on genuine altruists. It underscores that **transparency and authenticity** are vital for trust.

There's also a social learning aspect: If communities start recognizing patterns of "performative altruism," they might become better at noticing red flags. For instance, if someone is *too* self-promoting about their charity or if their family members seem oddly unhappy amid supposed domestic bliss, astute observers might not dismiss that so easily. The conversation could shift to include, "He does a lot of good, but I wonder if he's taking care of himself and his family too; that's important." If such awareness grows, it could gently pressure would-be communal narcissists to not neglect their families, since they can't count on automatic sainthood status from their deeds.

7.4 Cultural and Structural Factors

It's important to note that cultural norms differ. In some collectivist cultures, for example, the idea of sacrificing family time for community might be more expected, or extended family might step in to fill gaps (mitigating child neglect somewhat if relatives are close by). In other cultures, emphasis on the nuclear family is strong, so neglecting it is more uniformly condemned. However, even in family-centric cultures, if the person's external role is say religious or political, they might get leeway or excuses due to reverence for that role.

Institutionally, workplaces and organizations can either help or hinder. A progressive workplace might encourage work-life balance, subtly discouraging people from being absent parents (like offering paternity leave or expecting one to go home in evenings). But volunteer organizations or religious institutions often welcome over-commitment–they need volunteers, and someone saying "yes" to everything is seen as a godsend for them. They might unintentionally exploit that person's need for validation because it aligns with their need for labour. Rarely will a charity head say, "You've done enough, go home to your family." Instead, they'll likely keep accepting help. This is a structural factor–there are plenty of avenues that will eagerly consume a person's time and energy for good causes and never ask about the person's home life. Without checks, a person inclined to over-invest outside can find endless opportunities to do so, further **unbalancing their life**. Ideally, mentors or colleagues in those spaces would watch out for burnout or imbalance (for example, a church leader might gently tell a volunteer to spend Sunday afternoon with their kids instead of at the fourth church meeting of the week), but it's not common.

Societal narratives of the "hero" can also be problematic. We lionize those who go above and beyond, sometimes without asking at what cost. When someone is described as "giving 110%" or "she's always there for everyone," it sounds positive, but maybe no one can or should be always there for everyone. Perhaps at times we should question, "Does this person also take care of themselves and their own? Do they have downtime?" The notion of the self-sacrificing hero is deeply embedded in many cultures (the idea of martyrdom, even secular martyrdom, for a cause). Communal narcissists latch onto this narrative because it gives them purpose and applause. Society, by venerated such figures without scrutiny, provides fertile ground for them.

7.5 Towards Greater Awareness

For real change, society needs greater awareness of emotional neglect as a serious issue. As the British Journal of Psychiatry editorial argued, "*we must work towards raising public awareness about the signs and the mental health impact of emotional abuse and neglect*". If friends, extended family, teachers, and others are more educated about how a child who "has everything" materially might still be suffering due to lack of emotional presence from a parent, they might catch on sooner and offer support or intervention. If communities can handle the nuance that a person can do good things and do bad things (i.e., shedding black-and-white thinking), then they can hold their heroes accountable to being decent on all fronts, not just the public one.

For example, imagine a community where, when giving an award to someone, they also say, "We'd like to acknowledge their family for supporting them, and we urge all our volunteers to remember to take care of home as well." Even small acknowledgments like that set a tone that **family responsibilities are not to be neglected in the name of community service**. Or in faith communities, leaders could preach that one's first ministry is one's family, putting spiritual weight on that, to counteract any misinterpretation that only church work matters.

In terms of structural help, **family counselling services** could be more attuned to this pattern. Instead of waiting for a crisis, perhaps communities can encourage periodic family check-ins or workshops on balancing community involvement with family life. People who tend to overcommit could be gently confronted in a supportive way early on ("I notice you volunteer for everything. How is that affecting your time with your kids?"). Some might appreciate the chance to reflect, possibly feeling a bit trapped by their own compulsion to say yes.

Society also must accept that a tarnished public image of one person doesn't invalidate all the good work that was done. For instance, if a community leader is exposed as a bad parent, it doesn't mean the charity they ran is false. But there is often collateral damage—people might pull back support from a cause because of the personal failings of its figurehead. This is unfortunate, and communities face a delicate task of separating the value of the work from the value of the worker in these cases. Recognizing communal narcissism as a psychological issue might help: we can see them not as pure evil hypocrites (which can lead to total repudiation of everything associated with them) but as flawed individuals whose motivations were mixed. The cause they championed may still be valid, but they themselves need help or consequences.

A hopeful possibility is that as mental health conversations become more mainstream, terms like "narcissistic parent," "childhood emotional neglect," and "toxic family dynamics" gain currency in everyday discussion. This could empower more children (once grown) and spouses to label and speak about their experiences, which in turn educates the public. Memoirs or stories in media about such scenarios can raise awareness. Empathy might shift: instead of automatically applauding the public servant, people might more often ask, "I wonder how their family feels." Not in a cynical way, but in a holistic one.

Finally, **legal systems** typically don't intervene in emotional neglect unless it's extreme, but some jurisdictions include emotional harm in definitions of child welfare. If a spouse divorces citing emotional neglect, it might not influence settlements much compared to concrete abuse or adultery, etc. However, if patterns become clearer, perhaps custody evaluators and courts may consider whether a parent has been emotionally absent when figuring out a child's best interests. That is speculative and tricky to implement, but it's a thought on how societal institutions can confirm that aspect.

In conclusion, society has a dual role: it initially fuels the outward-focused person with admiration and permission to ignore home, but it can later also be the force that chastises and corrects. The key is shortening the gap between those two phases by fostering awareness. When communities value consistency of character (how you treat your family matters as much as how you treat others) and support those who speak up about hidden abuse or neglect, the duplicity has less room to fester. In the next chapter, we will synthesize insights from the psychological and social analysis we've done, and consider theoretical integrations and implications for change—how understanding these patterns can lead to better outcomes for families and communities alike.

Chapter 8: Theoretical Integration and Implications for Change

Having dissected this phenomenon from multiple angles—psychological, familial, and societal—we now integrate the insights and discuss broader theoretical frameworks as well as potential pathways to mitigate such situations. In this chapter, we revisit key theories (social validation, family systems, attachment theory, etc.) to see how they interconnect in explaining the duplicity of outward altruism and inward neglect. We also consider what can be done with this understanding: how might individuals, families, and communities apply this knowledge to foster healthier dynamics? The tone shifts toward a scholarly reflection on what has been learned and a forward-looking perspective on addressing the issue.

8.1 Integrating Social Validation Theory and Family Systems

At the heart of our analysis is a tension between two sources of validation: **societal validation vs. familial validation.** Social validation theory suggests people have a deep need for acknowledgment and acceptance from others. Family systems theory shows that a family functions best when members validate and support each other internally. In the cases we've discussed, the individual (parent/elder) chooses the external source to fulfil their needs at the expense of the internal source. They essentially **outsource their self-esteem** to the community, neglecting the feedback loop within the family that could also provide esteem and belonging.

Why does this happen for some individuals and not others? It could be a combination of personality predisposition and their own upbringing (perhaps they did not receive unconditional familial validation growing up, so they don't know how to either receive or give it now). Family systems theory, particularly Bowen's concept of **differentiation of self**, may offer insight. A well-differentiated person can maintain their sense of self while also being connected in relationships. A poorly differentiated person either becomes emotionally fused with others or emotionally cut off. The altruistic validation-seeker might be poorly differentiated: they are fused with the *audience's* opinion (overly influenced by it), and cut off from the emotional climate at home (unable to engage intimately without feeling overwhelmed or inadequate). So they oscillate between seeking fusion with society's regard and maintaining distance at home.

From a **systems perspective**, one could say the family became organized around the narcissistic or validation-seeking behaviour. In Minuchin's structural family theory terms, boundaries might have been inappropriately drawn: the community almost functions like a pseudo-family for the parent (with those outside relationships taking a priority that family should), meaning the **hierarchy of priorities is inverted**. Family systems therapy would attempt to realign this, putting spousal and parent-child subsystems back in proper order, and reducing the outside system's intrusion.

Social validation needs aren't inherently bad; they drive people to contribute to society. The key is **balance** and ensuring those needs don't override empathy and presence in one's primary relationships. Perhaps one integrative theoretical way to view it is through **Self-Determination Theory (SDT)** which differentiates between intrinsic and extrinsic motivations. The validation-seeker's altruism is largely extrinsically motivated (for approval, status). According to SDT, extrinsic goals (like fame or image) when prioritized over intrinsic ones (like close relationships, personal growth) are associated with lower well-being and more ill-being. This aligns with what we see: the person's pursuit, although it masquerades as something socially valued, is an extrinsic chase that correlates with dysfunction (unhappiness in their family, likely themselves never fully at peace either). Helping such a person might involve shifting toward more intrinsic motivation—finding genuine enjoyment in helping (not for praise) and finding genuine enjoyment in family connection (not just seeing it as duty or hindrance). In a sense, **internal validation (from within and from one's intimate circle) is more stable and healthier** than chasing constant external validation.

Additionally, we can integrate **attachment theory** here. A parent's behaviour is often transmitted from their own attachment experiences. If this outwardly altruistic parent had an insecure attachment, they might be playing out a pattern of seeking approval (anxious attachment to the "public") while avoidantly handling close relationships (because intimacy perhaps scares them due to fear of not being good enough). They may find the relative emotional distance of community interactions safer than the vulnerable, messy closeness of family life. The tragedy is they then pass on insecure attachment to their children, perpetuating a cycle of disconnection masked by busyness.

Another relevant theory is **Maslow's hierarchy of needs:** love/belonging and esteem are both needs. Ideally, one satisfies belonging (family love) and then gains esteem in healthy ways. But here, the person might skip addressing belonging at home and jump to esteem needs via outside achievements. Maslow would suggest that ignoring the belonging need (family love) leads to a hollow fulfilment of esteem—like building on a shaky foundation. No matter how much praise they get, an emptiness may remain (which is why narcissistic supply is never enough—they have a deficit only emotional connection can fill). Thus, they keep pushing for more admiration as a substitute. Recognizing this theoretically could inform therapy: one would work on healing that belonging need (maybe this person feels emotionally safer in crowds than one-on-one, which we must reverse).

In terms of **cognitive dissonance theory**, the parent might experience dissonance if confronted with their neglect, since it conflicts with their identity as a caring person. They tend to resolve dissonance by justifying their actions (moral licensing: "I do so much good, it's okay that I'm irritable at home") or by devaluing those who question them (the spouse or child is framed as overly sensitive, etc.). A therapeutic or corrective approach would be to gently induce dissonance in a constructive way: maybe have them hear from their child's perspective deeply (perhaps via family therapy sessions where the child can safely express hurt). If they can't rationalize that away, they might feel the discomfort needed to motivate change—realizing "I thought I was an amazing parent, but my child is deeply hurt; I must reconcile that." Not all will respond, but some could.

The concept of **identity** is also crucial. The person's ego identity got wrapped in the communal role (hence the term communal narcissism). They cherish "their status as givers". To adjust this, they'd need to expand or alter their identity to include being a nurturing parent or present spouse as equally valuable. Essentially, they need to derive pride from being there for their family, not just from public deeds. This might require societal reinforcement too: if communities equally praise "he's a great dad" as much as "he's great for the community," it helps. Identity shift can be slow, but midlife sometimes triggers it (some communal narcissists, as they age, realize they are not actually deeply loved, just admired, and that can spur a crisis).

From a family systems plus societal view, the whole network around such a person often needed to change for improvement. If the family alone tries to change but the community keeps rewarding the old behaviour, it's an uphill battle. Conversely, if community perceptions change (like a few friends intervene or a pastor calls out the importance of family time), and the family asserts needs, together those pressures could tip the balance.

8.2 Implications for Prevention and Change

Understanding these dynamics suggests several points of intervention:

For Individuals (the parents/elders themselves): Psychological interventions would aim at increasing self-awareness of motives. Tools like reflective journaling might help one notice "Am I doing this deed to help or to be seen helping?" Even communal narcissists sometimes can grasp that conceptually if willing. Therapy (individual) could focus on developing empathy—maybe trying perspective-taking exercises regarding their family. Sometimes, helping them connect their own childhood experiences (if they felt unloved) to what they are reenacting can be powerful (psychodynamic insight). That said, narcissistic individuals often resist therapy unless a crisis pushes them, but some might come if it's framed around "improving family relations" (as that can be seen as another achievement). Techniques from CBT could challenge their distorted beliefs ("If I don't do all these things, people won't respect me" - is that true, or can you be respected also for being a good parent?).

For Families (spouse/children): Prevention here means fostering open communication early on. If from the start, the spouse sets boundaries ("I support your volunteering, but we need a weekly date night" or "the kids need you at their bedtime most nights"), that can check extreme patterns. For children, educating them that a parent's lack of attention is not their fault is crucial (maybe through school counsellors or paediatricians who catch signs). In some cases, involving a third party (like a family therapist or respected elder) to mediate and make the parent listen is necessary. The family can also make a unified stand: e.g., an intervention where multiple members lovingly confront the person with specific examples of feeling neglected, combined with praise for what they do but stressing "*we need you too.*" This mirrors interventions used for addicts–here the "drug" is social praise.

For Communities: Community organizations can incorporate family-friendly policies. For example, if someone is spending excessive time volunteering, a leader could say, "We require volunteers to take at least one weekend off a month for family/personal time." It sounds odd, but some progressive organizations do worry about volunteer burnout and have guidelines like that. Recognitions like awards could include a note thanking the person's family explicitly, sending a subtle message that it's a team effort and the family's share matters. Community education via workshops or church sermons on topics like balancing service and home life could plant seeds.

In schools or youth programs, including content on emotional health might allow kids of such parents to speak up or at least be validated by an adult that "your feelings matter." If a teacher or counsellor learns a child feels a parent is "nicer to everyone else than to me," that's a red flag to gently address perhaps in parent-teacher conversation or referral to counselling.

Policy and Society: While emotional neglect is hard to legislate, increased funding for family counselling and parenting programs could help. New parents, especially those who are very career or community driven, might receive help from parenting workshops that emphasize emotional presence. Sometimes high-achieving individuals treat parenting like a checklist (provide, pay for things) and don't realize the intangible emotional tasks needed. If paediatricians or social workers during early childhood can counsel parents about tuning in to their child, that might pre-empt some neglect for those who simply lack the skill (not necessarily full narcissists, but busy individuals who might drift into this pattern).

In workplaces, acknowledging that employees have families and encouraging balance can indirectly curb the formation of these patterns. If the altruistic parent's day job was also extremely demanding, an employer that enforces reasonable hours indirectly helps them have bandwidth for family. So, the general movement towards work-life balance aligns here.

Therapeutic Models: There are appearing therapeutic frameworks like **Internal Family Systems (IFS)** (not to be confused with general family systems theory) which could be intriguingly applicable. IFS would look at a person as having parts, perhaps one part desperately seeking external approval and another vulnerable part that feels unworthy (possibly shielded by the first). It might try to get the over-achiever part to relax and allow the vulnerable part to get healing (maybe that vulnerable part is the one that didn't get love in childhood and ironically is causing the approval chasing). If the person can self-validate that vulnerable part, the need to get it from outside might lessen.

Community-level Narcissism Awareness: Our society has in recent years become more aware of terms like gaslighting and narcissistic abuse (through social media, etc.). While pop psychology can oversimplify, this awareness can empower victims (spouses/children) and hold perpetrators more accountable. The more people realize that someone can smile and help you but still harm their family, the more they might support the family if issues arise.

One interesting concept from positive psychology is **"Healthy Selfishness"** as contrasted with pathological altruism. Encouraging a healthy dose of self-care and personal/family prioritization might sound counterintuitive in an altruism context, but it may lead to more sustainable and sincere altruism. Barbara Oakley's work on **pathological altruism** reminds us that good intentions can go awry and hurt oneself or one's group. If an altruist is made aware that neglecting their family is a form of harm that ultimately undermines the goodness of their actions (because causing suffering at home is not ethically outweighed by helping others), they may recalibrate how they define altruism. In ethics, there's the concept of **"moral integrity"** – being consistent in principles across contexts. Invoking moral integrity might appeal to their desire to be a genuinely good person: "If you want to do the most good, shouldn't you ensure those closest to you are not suffering due to your actions? " Charity starts at home ."

Future Research: From an academic perspective, more research could be directed at measuring effects of communal narcissism on family outcomes. We have pieces (like the PT references and some anecdotal or case studies) but quantitative studies might involve assessing children of people high on communal narcissism scales for outcomes like depression, or examining marital satisfaction in those relationships. Studies could also test interventions (maybe group therapy for spouses of communal narcissists, akin to Al-Anon for families of addicts, could provide support and strategies). Social psychology experiments could test if reminding someone of family commitments before an opportunity to help others influences their choice (basically priming intrinsic/familial cues vs extrinsic/public ones).

The integration of theory thus provides a comprehensive understanding: Social validation needs and narcissistic traits explain the behaviour; family systems theory explains the ripple effect on family structure; attachment theory and emotional neglect literature explain the impact on children; sociological perspective explains how community feedback loops reinforce or challenge the behaviour. This holistic view implies that addressing the issue also requires a comprehensive approach—one that considers individual change, family healing, and societal norms.

8.3 Towards Healthier Family and Community Dynamics

In terms of concluding implications, one theme appears: **balance and authenticity**. Encouraging individuals to live more authentically means aligning their public persona with their private one. If society values authenticity, people might feel less need to hide flaws behind good deeds. Normalizing the fact that being a good parent/spouse is as praiseworthy as being a good community leader could shift personal priorities organically.

For the families affected, it's critical to confirm the children's and spouse's experiences. If a child or spouse finds the courage to speak about this duplicity, believing them is crucial. Mental health professionals should take it seriously—just because a parent appears wonderful doesn't mean the child's complaints are false (a trap even therapists can fall into without awareness).

We also might highlight positive examples of people who changed. Perhaps there are stories (fictional or real) of a workaholic or communal narcissist who realized it and reformed—showcasing that change is possible. Those could serve as templates or inspiration.

In community ethics, perhaps including family well-being as part of evaluating leadership is important. For example, some organizations when hiring consider not just a candidate's resume but also if they demonstrate healthy interpersonal skills and balance. It's tricky because one's private life is private, but extreme cases do spill over. If a leader's family is in crisis due to their neglect, eventually it can affect the organization (e.g., scandals or sudden burnout). So it's in organizations' interest too.

In summary, the integration of theories underscores that the phenomenon of outward altruism and inward neglect is multi-faceted. It is at once an individual psychological issue (often rooted in unmet validation needs or personality disorder), a family issue (causing systemic dysfunction and trauma), and a social issue (influenced by cultural values and community responses). Consequently, solutions must work on all those levels. Building awareness, fostering open dialogue, and shifting values toward a more holistic notion of altruism (one that doesn't sacrifice one's own family in the process) are key steps.

Chapter 9: Conclusion of the Perspective

The exploration of parents and elders who seek societal validation through altruistic behaviour while neglecting their own families reveals a complex interplay of personal psychology, family dynamics, and social influence. We have seen that these individuals often fit the profile of **communal narcissism**–they derive self-worth from the image of being caring and helpful yet paradoxically lack genuine empathy for those closest to them. Their need for external approval, as explained by social validation theory and contingent self-esteem, drives them to prioritize the admiration of strangers over the love of their own children and spouses. This creates a painful **duplicity**: a front-stage persona celebrated by the community, and a backstage reality of emotional neglect, manipulation, or abuse within the family.

The psychological and emotional ramifications of this pattern are profound. Children raised in such an environment suffer **childhood**

emotional neglect, which research has linked to depression, anxiety, low self-esteem, and difficulty in later relationships. They grow up feeling unimportant and unseen, often blaming themselves for the lack of parental warmth. The example of the daughter whose communal narcissist mother was "*cold and unloving*" despite her public kindness illustrates the lasting impact: even into adulthood, that daughter's emotional well-being was compromised until the truth was acknowledged. Spouses, too, endure chronic loneliness and erosion of self-worth, often feeling like they "*walk on eggshells*" around a partner who dismisses their needs. Many develop symptoms of trauma from years of **gaslighting, invalidation, and emotional abandonment**. In short, the family members experience significant harm—harm that is often invisible to or ignored by the outside world.

Family systems theory illuminated how an entire family can become organized around the validation-seeking behaviour of one member, leading to dysfunctional roles and communication patterns. We found phenomena like the *scapegoat child* who bears blame for family issues, the *hero child* who overachieves to compensate, and the spouse who becomes an enabler or emotionally withdraws. The **central functions of family—emotional support, mutual care, healthy boundaries—are subverted** in these situations. Instead of being a source of unconditional love and validation, the family environment revolves around maintaining the parent's facade or coping with their neglect. This systemic view reinforces that the problem is not isolated to individual relationships but pervades the whole family unit, with each member adapting (often maladaptively) to the skewed dynamic.

On the societal level, we discussed how community perceptions can at first **reinforce the harmful behaviour**. The *halo effect* leads people to assume that a publicly caring person must be a good spouse/parent as well. Social accolades and praise serve as positive reinforcement for the parent, effectively **rewarding their neglect** (since their time away from family yields admiration . This collective blindness or denial means that children's or spouses' voices are often marginalized—few believe them or they are labelled as ungrateful if they dare complain. However, when the facade eventually cracks (as often it does, under the weight of accumulated evidence or a breaking point in the family), the backlash from society can be severe, and the once-admired individual may face a dramatic loss of reputation. We see the arc of **initial idealization to eventual devaluation** not only in personal relationships with narcissists but in the community's relationship to them as well. This reflects the hypocritical nature of the setup—once hypocrisy is revealed, society feels "duped" and reacts strongly.

Incorporating relevant theories enriched our understanding. The concept of contingent self-worth explained why validation-hungry parents behave this way: their self-esteem is contingent on others' approval, leading them to aggressively pursue praise at the expense of more stable sources of self-worth. Narcissistic supply theory likewise showed that these altruistic acts function to gain narcissistic supply (admiration) rather than arising from true altruism. We saw that moral licensing allowed these individuals to internally justify neglectful behaviour ("I've done good, so I can relax my moral obligations elsewhere"). Family systems and attachment theories helped explain the damage to children's development and the perpetuation of insecurity and dysfunction across generations. By triangulating these theoretical perspectives, we get a comprehensive picture: a personality prone to external validation meets a family context that fails to correct it and a society that initially rewards it, producing a perfect storm of outward virtue and private vice.

The critical and scholarly tone of this essay has intentionally juxtaposed the observable behaviours with underlying motives and consequences. By citing contemporary research and expert analyses, we validated that **emotional neglect is as real and harmful as more visible forms of maltreatment**. This is a key point: just because the harm is done through omission (failing to provide love) and behind closed doors, it does not make it any less legitimate of a problem. Indeed, as one source noted, emotional abuse/neglect is *"among the most prevalent"* forms of child maltreatment and has extensive negative impacts. Therefore, shining a light on this hidden issue is important for both academia and public discourse.

In reflecting on solutions and implications, we recognized that addressing such situations requires interventions at multiple levels:

- **Individually**, these parents/elders would benefit from therapy or coaching to build insight into their motivations and learn to value their family relationships. Learning to derive self-worth from within (or from healthy family interactions) rather than constant social applause is a crucial shift. Developing empathy is another core goal. There are indications that some communal narcissists can change if they become aware of the discrepancy between their self-image and others' perception, and if they truly grasp the pain, they are causing their loved ones. Techniques like perspective-taking, empathy training, or even specific programs for narcissistic behaviours (some emerging group therapies or work by specialists like Dr. Craig Malkin, etc.) could be applied.
- **For families**, involving a family therapist to reorganize family dynamics can be instrumental. For example, in therapy, the spouse and children's feelings could be validated and the parent gently confronted with their experiences, bridging the gap of understanding. Strengthening the spousal subsystem (so the married couple present a united front and share power) can help counter the narcissist's domination. Teaching children that their parent's behaviour is not their fault can mitigate internalized trauma. In some cases, setting firm boundaries or, if all else fails, the spouse may choose separation to protect themselves and the children from

further harm—though difficult, it sometimes leads the neglectful parent to face consequences and possibly reform.

- **At the community level**, the essay argued for raising awareness and not idolizing public figures unconditionally. Communities and workplaces can encourage more balanced lives. By acknowledging and rewarding people for being good family members (not just for public deeds), society can send a message that success at home is an essential part of overall virtue. Public institutions (schools, churches, etc.) can provide support to families showing signs of this issue—perhaps offering parenting workshops that highlight the importance of emotional presence or providing safe channels for spouses/children to seek help without fear of public shame. Ultimately, a cultural shift to recognize emotional neglect and hold individuals accountable in both spheres of life—public and private—would create an environment where this duplicity is less likely to thrive.

In closing, it is worth emphasizing that altruism and caring for others are wonderful traits that societies should encourage, but not at the **expense of one's own family's well-being**. True altruism does not require the sacrifice of those who depend on us. As the adage goes, "*Charity begins at home.*" This does not mean charity should end at home, but that one's duty to one's family is foundational and should accompany, not be supplanted by, duty to the broader community. Parents and elders who genuinely wish to do good must strive for consistency: to be kind, compassionate, and attentive not only to neighbours and strangers, but also—indeed especially—to their own children, spouses, and aging parents. By aligning their private behaviour with their public image, they achieve integrity, and the admiration they receive will be grounded, not a facade.

For those who have suffered under such duplicity, this essay serves to validate their experiences and bring them to scholarly attention.

The emotional neglect they endured is real, and the confusion and hurt caused by seeing a loved one's compassion freely given to others but denied at home is a deep wound, one that deserves recognition and healing. Going forward, a critical and compassionate scholarly eye on this subject can inform both prevention and intervention strategies, ensuring that **outward altruism is paired with inward genuineness**. In an ideal scenario, the nurturing energy of these individuals could be distributed more evenly illuminating both the public sphere and the home with the same warmth. Families would then cease to be collateral damage of public virtue and instead become direct beneficiaries of their loved one's kindness. In turn, a supportive family could further empower the individual's altruistic efforts in the community, creating a positive cycle in place of the destructive one we have analysed.

This phenomenon of outwardly altruistic yet privately neglectful parents/elders is a cautionary tale of imbalance—of esteem needs overshadowing belonging needs, of image overtaking substance. It challenges us to think more holistically about character and virtue. A truly good person cares for those dependent on them as well as for the wider world; there is no inconsistency between the two. By understanding the psychological drivers and devastating effects of this inconsistency, we can better identify it, address it, and ultimately foster a culture where altruism is not performative but sincere, emanating from well-tended homes to a better-tended world.

Conclusion: Coming Home to Yourself — The Full Circle of Psyche

"You don't arrive at healing. You return to it – again and again – until it becomes your way of living."

~ Anonymous

If you've made it here, you didn't just read a book.

You took your psyche on a pilgrimage — through memory, emotion, survival, rebellion, redemption, and reinvention.

This wasn't a book about self-help.

This was a book about **self-return.**

You met your mind.

You confronted your past.

You danced with your shadows.

You broke cycles that didn't start with you — but were brave enough to end with you.

Each chapter was a **threshold** — and you crossed them all.

🧠 **Chapter 1: The Mirror**

You began with the **fundamentals of the psyche** — not just as a concept, but as a living, breathing force. You learned that the mind is not just a machine — it's a **map** of every story you've lived, inherited, suppressed, or silenced.

🧠 **Chapter 2: The Conditioning**

You unwrapped the **scripts you never signed up for** — the beliefs you were taught to believe, the roles you were rewarded for playing, the truths you learned to bury. You understood that conditioning isn't your fault – but unlearning it *is* your responsibility.

Chapter 3: The Inner Critic

You met the voice that has whispered lies in your head for years. The one that said, "Not enough," "Too late," "Who do you think you are?" And you didn't shut it up – you understood it. You took back the mic.

Chapter 4: The Trauma Codes

You looked pain in the eye. You named what others told you to forget. You redefined trauma – not as what happened *to* you, but what stayed **within** you. You didn't just seek healing – you *decoded it.*

Chapter 5: Brutal Truths About Human Behaviour

You stopped sugar-coating. You saw that love can coexist with manipulation. That brilliance can exist in brokenness. That healing demands **radical honesty** – and you chose truth over comfort.

Chapter 6: Healing in Real Time

You learned that healing isn't linear, it's **seasonal**. You don't "get over it" – you *move through it.* You now know that progress isn't always visible – sometimes it's choosing not to repeat the pattern, even when it's still familiar.

Chapter 7: The Masks We Wear

You shed your performance armour. You examined every identity you wore to belong, to survive, to be praised. And one by one, you dropped them – until what was left was **authenticity without apology.**

Chapter 8: Emotional Intelligence in a Numb World

You took emotions off mute. You began feeling fully again – not because it's easy, but because it's **real.** You saw that EQ is not softness – it's your **superpower** in a world addicted to disconnection.

🌑 Chapter 9: The Shadow Self

You went into the basement of your being. You made peace with the parts you once banished. You saw that integration is more powerful than perfection – and that **wholeness comes when nothing inside you must hide.**

🗣 Chapter 10: The Inner Voice

You rewrote the narrative in your head. You silenced the echoes of your critics, your wounds, and your fears. And in their place, you planted a voice that speaks like a lover, not a judge.

💣 Chapter 11: Self-Sabotage

You faced the part of you that blocks your own light. You saw that sabotage isn't stupidity – it's protection. And you rewired it. With awareness. With compassion. With boundaries. With truth.

🧸 Chapter 12: Reparenting the Inner Child

You returned to the child inside you who never got to feel safe. You listened. You held them. You gave them what the world couldn't. And now, they no longer cry alone.

🛡 Chapter 13: Emotional Safety

You realized that love without safety isn't intimacy – it's anxiety. You saw that safety is the soil where trust, truth, and healing grow. And you decided to be that soil for yourself – and for others.

🧱 Chapter 14: Boundaries

You stopped bleeding to make others comfortable. You understood that "no" is a holy word. That "enough" is a declaration. And that **the most sacred relationships are not boundary-less – they are boundary-wise.**

🔥 Chapter 15: Resilience Rewired

You stopped romanticizing strength. You learned that resilience is *not* about pretending nothing hurts – it's about building a life that lets you feel everything and still rise.

⚠️ Chapter 16: The Anatomy of Self-Betrayal

You traced every moment you abandoned yourself to stay accepted. And you made a promise: *Never again will I silence my truth to keep someone else comfortable.*

🔎 Chapter 17: Identity, Integrity & Becoming Who You Truly Are

You stopped confusing who you *were trained to be* with who you *are becoming.* You realized that identity is not fixed – it is reclaimed. Rebuilt. Rewritten. By you, for you.

🧠💥 So, What Now?

You don't go back to your old life after a book like this.

You don't go back to faking fine, over-giving, shrinking, or pretending.

You go forward:

- With courage
- With clarity
- With compassion
- With *consciousness*

You are not who you were when you picked this book up.

You are **the author of your next chapter**.

You are not the broken one.

You are the brave one.

You are not here to be liked.

You are here to be **lit up** from within.

You are not your pain.

You are the one **who turned pain into prophecy.**

🔥 **Final Words:**

Let this book not just sit on your bookshelf.

Let it be your **mirror**, your **manual**, your **mission.**

Let this be the moment you decided:

"No more playing small. No more betraying myself. No more waiting for permission to fully be."

"This is my mind. My story. My psyche. My legacy."

You're home now.

And from here – everything changes.

Forever with you,

Victor Chatterjee

Legacy Letter to the Reader

– from Victor Chatterjee

Dear Reader,

If you've made it this far, you didn't just finish a book.

You walked through fire.

You wrestled with shadows.

You dared to remember parts of yourself the world asked you to forget.

And that makes you family.

This wasn't written as a product.

It was written as a pulse – a heartbeat from mine to yours.

I didn't write this as an expert. I wrote it as a man who's broken, rebuilt, fallen again, screamed into pillows, questioned his worth, almost quit on himself more times than he'd admit – and still chose to stay.

I've walked through shame.

I've tasted the ache of loneliness surrounded by people.

I've smiled at board meetings while feeling like an imposter inside.

I've been praised for strength... while silently drowning.

And I know – I *know* – that healing isn't always loud.

Sometimes, it's choosing to get out of bed.

Sometimes, it's saying no.

Sometimes, it's showing up when you'd rather disappear.

If there's one thing, I want you to take from this book – it's this:

You are not too late.

You are not too broken.

You are not too sensitive.

You are not too much.

And you never needed to earn your worth.

Your story isn't behind you – it's inside you.

And what lives inside you is *still writing itself.*

Maybe you were silenced, overlooked, made to feel like your softness was a weakness.

But I promise you – your softness is your strength.

Your truth is not a liability – it's your legacy.

If no one's told you lately:

I'm proud of you.

For surviving.

For choosing growth.

For choosing yourself.

For choosing to not abandon your light – even when others asked you to dim it.

This isn't goodbye.

This is an invitation.

Live louder.

Love deeper.

Heal forward.

And leave this world more honest than you found it.

With reverence, resilience, and a rebel heart,

Victor Chatterjee

Kolkata, India.

Bibliography

Adams, E.L., Smith, D., Caccavale, L.J. and Bean, M.K., 2021. Parents are stressed! Patterns of parent stress across COVID-19. *Frontiers in Psychiatry*, 12, p.626456.

Andréassi, J.L., 2010. *Psychophysiology: Human behavior and physiological response*. Psychology Press.

Bancroft, L., Silverman, J.G. and Ritchie, D., 2011. *The batterer as parent: Addressing the impact of domestic violence on family dynamics*. Sage Publications.

Beck, D.E. and Cowan, C.C., 2014. *Spiral dynamics: Mastering values, leadership and change*. John Wiley & Sons.

Blanchard, L.T., Gurka, M.J. and Blackman, J.A., 2006. Emotional, developmental, and behavioral health of American children and their families: A report from the 2003 National Survey of Children's Health. *Pediatrics*, 117(6), pp.e1202–e1212.

Bond, T.G. and Fox, C.M., 2013. *Applying the Rasch model: Fundamental measurement in the human sciences*. Psychology Press.

Boszormenyi-Nagy, I., 2014. *Invisible loyalties*. Routledge.

Cabrera, N., Tamis-LeMonda, C.S., Bradley, R.H., Hofferth, S. and Lamb, M.E., 2000. Fatherhood in the twenty-first century. *Child Development*, 71(1), pp.127–136.

Cauce, A.M., Domenech-Rodríguez, M., Paradise, M., Cochran, B.N., Shea, J.M., Srebnik, D. and Baydar, N., 2002. Cultural and contextual influences in mental health help seeking: A focus on ethnic minority youth. *Journal of Consulting and Clinical Psychology*, 70(1), p.44.

Chandra, A., Martin, L.T., Hawkins, S.A. and Richardson, A., 2010. The impact of parental deployment on child social and emotional functioning: Perspectives of school staff. *Journal of Adolescent Health*, 46(3), pp.218–223.

Chung, G., Lanier, P. and Wong, P.Y.J., 2022. Mediating effects of parental stress on harsh parenting and parent–child relationship during coronavirus (COVID-19) pandemic in Singapore. *Journal of Family Violence*, 37(5), pp.801–812.

Cost, K.T., Crosbie, J., Anagnostou, E., Birken, C.S., Charach, A., Monga, S., Kelley, E., Nicolson, R., Maguire, J.L., Burton, C.L. and Schachar, R.J., 2021. Mostly worse, occasionally better: Impact of COVID-19 pandemic on the mental health of Canadian children and adolescents. *European Child & Adolescent Psychiatry*, pp.1–14.

Cripps, K. and Zyromski, B., 2009. Adolescents' psychological well-being and perceived parental involvement: Implications for parental involvement in middle schools. *RMLE Online*, 33(4), pp.1–13.

Darling, N., 2005. Participation in extracurricular activities and adolescent adjustment: Cross-sectional and longitudinal findings. *Journal of Youth and Adolescence*, 34, pp.493–505.

Deb, S., Strodl, E. and Sun, H., 2015. Academic stress, parental pressure, anxiety and mental health among Indian high school students. *International Journal of Psychology and Behavioral Science*, 5(1), pp.26–34.

DeSocio, J. and Hootman, J., 2004. Children's mental health and school success. *The Journal of School Nursing*, 20(4), pp.189–196.

Duncan, L.G., Coatsworth, J.D. and Greenberg, M.T., 2009. A model of mindful parenting: Implications for parent–child relationships and prevention research. *Clinical Child and Family Psychology Review*, 12, pp.255–270.

Farb, A.F. and Matjasko, J.L., 2012. Recent advances in research on school-based extracurricular activities and adolescent development. *Developmental Review*, 32(1), pp.1–48.

Feldman, A.F. and Matjasko, J.L., 2005. The role of school-based extracurricular activities in adolescent development: A comprehensive review and future directions. *Review of Educational Research*, 75(2), pp.159–210.

Fegert, J.M., Vitiello, B., Plener, P.L. and Clemens, V., 2020. Challenges and burden of the Coronavirus 2019 (COVID-19) pandemic for child and adolescent mental health: A narrative review to highlight clinical and research needs in the acute phase and the long return to normality. *Child and Adolescent Psychiatry and Mental Health*, 14, pp.1–11.

Fiske, S.T., 2018. *Social beings: Core motives in social psychology*. John Wiley & Sons.

Fredricks, J.A., 2012. Extracurricular participation and academic outcomes: Testing the over-scheduling hypothesis. *Journal of Youth and Adolescence*, 41, pp.295–306.

Gadermann, A.C., Thomson, K.C., Richardson, C.G., Gagné, M., McAuliffe, C., Hirani, S. and Jenkins, E., 2021. Examining the impacts of the COVID-19 pandemic on family mental health in Canada: Findings from a national cross-sectional study. *BMJ Open*, 11(1), p.e042871.

Grolnick, W.S. and Pomerantz, E.M., 2009. Issues and challenges in studying parental control: Toward a new conceptualization. *Child Development Perspectives*, 3(3), pp.165–170.

Ho, M.K., Rasheed, J.M. and Rasheed, M.N., 2003. *Family therapy with ethnic minorities*. Sage Publications.

Kite, M. and Whitley, B.E., 2012. *Principles of research in behavioral science*. Routledge.

Lerner, R.M., 2018. *Concepts and theories of human development.* Routledge.

Logan, D.E. and King, C.A., 2001. Parental facilitation of adolescent mental health service utilization: A conceptual and empirical review. *Clinical Psychology: Science and Practice*, 8(3), p.319.

Paloutzian, R.F. and Park, C.L., eds., 2014. *Handbook of the psychology of religion and spirituality*. Guilford Publications.

Panchal, U., Salazar de Pablo, G., Franco, M., Moreno, C., Parellada, M., Arango, C. and Fusar-Poli, P., 2023. The impact of COVID-19 lockdown on child and adolescent mental health: Systematic review. *European Child & Adolescent Psychiatry*, 32(7), pp.1151–1177.

Panksepp, J., 2004. *Affective neuroscience: The foundations of human and animal emotions*. Oxford University Press.

Reis, H.T., Collins, W.A. and Berscheid, E., 2000. The relationship context of human behavior and development. *Psychological Bulletin*, 126(6), p.844.

Robbins, S.P. and DeCenzo, D.A., 2008. *Fundamentals of management: Essential concepts and applications*. Prentice Hall.

Samji, H., Wu, J., Ladak, A., Vossen, C., Stewart, E., Dove, N., Long, D. and Snell, G., 2022. Mental health impacts of the COVID-19 pandemic on children and youth – a systematic review. *Child and Adolescent Mental Health*, 27(2), pp.173–189.

Singh, S., Roy, D., Sinha, K., Parveen, S., Sharma, G. and Joshi, G., 2020. Impact of COVID-19 and lockdown on mental health of children and adolescents: A narrative review with recommendations. *Psychiatry Research*, 293, p.113429.

Stewart, M., Shizha, E., Makwarimba, E., Spitzer, D., Khalema, E.N. and Nsaliwa, C.D., 2011. Challenges and barriers to services for immigrant seniors in Canada: "You are among others but you feel alone". *International Journal of Migration, Health and Social Care*, 7(1), pp.16–32.

Törneke, N., 2010. *Learning RFT: An introduction to relational frame theory and its clinical application*. New Harbinger Publications.

Wang, M.T. and Sheikh-Khalil, S., 2014. Does parental involvement matter for student achievement and mental health in high school?. *Child Development*, 85(2), pp.610–625.

Zahra, S.A., Hayton, J.C., Neubaum, D.O., Dibrell, C. and Craig, J., 2008. Culture of family commitment and strategic flexibility: The moderating effect of stewardship. *Entrepreneurship Theory and Practice*, 32(6), pp.1035–1054.

Self Note Page: